Subprime Meltdown
From U.S. Liquidity Crisis
To Global Recession

Written by Charles Brownell
Justine Brownell, Editor

About the author

Charles has a Bachelor of Science in Finance from the University of Illinois, Champaign Urbana, and has been involved in the real estate business for more than 25 years.

He purchased his first real estate property in 1982. Since that time he's owned a total of 17 residential rental units. He has also bought and sold a few single-family properties: a home for rehab, a teardown for new construction and a vacant lot for new construction.

Copyright © 2008 Charles Brownell

All rights reserved.

No portion of this book may be reproduced in any form or by any means without the express written permission from the author.

Table of Contents

Chapter		Page
	Preface	5
1.	Subprime – What is it?	12
2.	The Role of Congress and The Federal Reserve	15
3.	History Repeats Itself	23
4.	Exploding ARMs	26
5.	Evolution of the Mortgage Business, Securitization and CDO's	32
6.	The Magic of Wall Street	43
7.	Scope of the Problem	46
8.	Why Subprime	51
9.	Victims and Losers	57
10.	Frauds and Scams	66
11.	A Typical Subprime Situation	74
12.	Credit Rating Agencies	91
13.	The Forecast	94
14.	Where Do We Go From Here?	103
15.	What Conclusions Can Be Drawn?	111
	Bibliography	115

Preface

This book is a general examination of the subprime mortgage process: how it works and how it has been abused.

It is a collection of analyses, stories, analogies and experiences about the real estate business, the mortgage business and the subprime market in particular.

The experiences and stories come from a variety of sources. Some are my own while others I've heard from friends and business associates, and some are fiction to illustrate a point.

This book will help you understand the big picture. You don't need to be a financial genius to understand the issues and ramifications. Some things you won't see in this book:

- You won't see hard to understand formulas.

- It isn't filled with technical jargon.

- There are no esoteric theories to explain what has happened in the subprime market. We will not explore the relationship between the Phillips curve and FOMC policy.

From the borrower's perspective, I believe the mortgage process has gotten completely out of control. There are hidden costs (yield spreads – explained later) and hidden agendas. Who does the mortgage broker really work for? He most certainly does not work for the buyer.

I also believe the out-of-control mortgage process is the primary reason for the subprime meltdown. Lenders packed subprime mortgage with exorbitant fees that borrowers had no hope of ever being able to repay.

To insure against a repeat of the subprime meltdown in the future we need better transparency in our mortgage process and our mortgage documents. It is almost impossible to decipher what you are signing when you buy a home.

If you are a homeowner and you used a mortgage broker to obtain your mortgage take a look at your closing documents. If there was a yield spread premium in there, chances are you paid that amount to your mortgage broker as a commission plus his regular commission.

Even if you know about the yield spread premium you may not be able to find it in your loan documents. Often it is buried in the mortgage amortization or hidden in the prepayment penalty.

Even with a trusted advisor or legal counsel, are you really certain about the details of everything you've signed when closing on a real estate loan? I'd venture to say that less than 1% of all borrowers ever bother to read their entire mortgage package – either before or after closing.

Even after closing most people simply file the documents and forget about them. They know how much they're supposed to pay each month. They've got enough on their plates with moving and decorating a new home.

Many people forgot that they signed up for an adjustable rate mortgage that would increase their mortgage payment dramatically in a couple of years or that they've got a pre-payment penalty if they decide to refinance.

When the rate does adjust and the payment skyrockets, they dig out that paperwork, thinking this can't be right, but sure enough there it is in black and white. Sometimes the pre-payment penalty is so large that it wipes out all their equity making refinancing impossible. They're stuck with a high interest loan.

Unfortunately that's the situation many subprime borrowers found themselves in and one of the reasons for our subprime meltdown. Those borrowers can no longer afford to make their mortgage payment and they can't afford to refinance or they can't find a lender willing to refinance their loan.

In the final analysis the subprime crisis came about because of greed, stupidity, fraud, overconfidence, arrogance and ignorance. I'll provide examples for each of those during the course of this book.

Here are some important numbers you'll see in this book. These are numbers that we hear regularly on the radio and read in our daily newspapers as I write this in 2008. You can also find these numbers in the governmental websites listed on page 9, or you can google them for more in-depth information.

- U.S. Household Net Worth (assets - liabilities) = a little less than $60 trillion (the Federal Reserve released their quarterly report at the beginning of June ' 08 showing a decline in household net worth for the first time in 5 years).

- U.S. Gross Domestic Product = $14 trillion

- U.S. Home Equity = $14 trillion

- U.S. Household debt, not including mortgages = $14 trillion

- Total Mortgages Outstanding = $9 trillion

- U.S. Homeowners = 80 million
    - That equals 70% of all households
    - 50 million homeowners have mortgages

- U.S. Homeowner foreclosures - estimated 2 million as of June 2008

- U.S. Homeowners who are behind on their mortgage payments – estimated 5 million

For the sake of simplicity I've rounded all numbers. I believe the data is accurate enough for the purposes of this discussion.

While we're on the subject of numbers, the mortgage payment information in the examples comes from my calculator and once again I've rounded all numbers.

Unless otherwise stated, the statistics and estimates are my own best guesses based upon information gathered from various governmental sources.

- The U.S. Department of Treasury http://www.ustreas.gov

- The U.S. Department of Housing and Urban Development http://www.huduser.org

- The Bureau of Economic Development http://www.bea.gov/

- The Federal Reserve http://www.federalreserve.gov

- The U.S. Government Printing Office http://www.access.gpo.gov

- The New York Federal Reserve http://www.newyorkfed.org

- Federal Financial Institutions Examination Council http://www.ffiec.gov

- The U.S. Census Bureau http://www.census.gov

- The Federal Deposit Insurance Corporation http://www.FDIC.gov

The FDIC!? What does the FDIC have to do with reporting on mortgages? I have no idea, but here's the URL for the data on mortgage volume (by the time you read this I hope the link is still good). http://www.fdic.gov/bank/analytical/regional/ro20062q/na/2006_summer04.html

Speaking of URL's and out of date links, since this book is not a research report or statistical analysis, for the most part I've decided to leave specific references for sources of data out of the book.

The stories contain only fictional characters – any relation to someone living or dead is purely coincidental. By no means do I mean to suggest that anyone I know has intentionally done anything illegal or unethical.

This book contains references to very large numbers – millions, billions and trillions of dollars. I always like to put things in perspective. Let's see how those really big numbers would look in terms of time.

- A million seconds is equal to approximately 12 days.

- A billion seconds is equal to 31 years.

- A trillion seconds is equal to 31,700 years.

Here's another way to look at it. Suppose you spent $1 every second. That is equal to spending $60 every minute; it would take you 31,700 years to spend $1 trillion dollars.

Let me put it another way.

The first Brownell to arrive on the shores of America was Thomas Brownell. He sailed to America in 1638 on the ship Whale, landing in Braintree, Massachusetts.

Thomas is the ancestor of most of the Brownell's in Canada and the United States. I am one of his descendants and an <u>eleventh generation</u> Brownell here in America.

It has been exactly 370 years since Thomas arrived on the shores of America. That is an average of 33 years between generations. If we were to apply the same rule of 33 years between generations, a trillion seconds would equal 960 generations.

Five generations ago we didn't have electricity, airplanes, automobiles, indoor plumbing or any of life's modern conveniences.

I can't imagine what the world will look like in another five generations, let alone nine generations, 96 generations or 960 generations!

You get the idea. A trillion of anything is an incomprehensibly large number.

I hope this book sheds some light on our financial institutions, the mortgage process, things that can go wrong, what to look out for, what to avoid, and how to protect yourself and your money.

Chapter 1
Subprime – What is it?

"A bank is a place where they lend you an umbrella in fair weather and ask for it back when it rains."

-Robert Frost

'Subprime' is a financial term used to identify borrowers who don't qualify for a 'prime' loan.

So what's a prime loan? A prime loan is a loan that charges the prime interest rate, also known as the 'prime rate'. Typically the prime rate is the interest rate charged to financial institutions' best customers. The prime rate is published in the business section of your local newspaper.

Sometimes customers with very high credit scores (explained below) pay less than prime. If you have a credit score over 800 you are probably going to pay prime minus .25% or .5%.

How do financial institutions distinguish between prime and subprime? If you have a credit score below 620, you are a subprime borrower.

What's a credit score? Your credit score is a number that represents your ability to pay your financial obligations. To calculate your credit score credit rating agencies take a number of factors into account including payment history and credit availability vs. credit used. The most popular credit score is from a company called Fair Isaac Corporation (they use the abbreviation FICO). The highest FICO credit score available is 850 and the lowest is 300. You can get a copy of your credit report for free once each year by contacting www.annualcreditreport.com.

So what can you expect if you are a subprime borrower? You can expect to pay a higher interest rate and higher fees for a loan. You can also expect to get turned down if your credit score is too low.

Subprime fees have traditionally been excessive, with most of the cost going to commissions. It isn't uncommon to see fees on subprime loans exceed 5% of the value of the loan. If the borrower only puts 5% down they'll end up with no equity in the property. True, they can add all those fees to the mortgage, but they still end up with no equity.

How does the prime rate relate to the interest rate for subprime borrowers?

A popular loan type is the 'adjustable rate mortgage' (ARM). The interest rate 'floats' with the prime rate or London Interbank Offered Rate (LIBOR). By floating, it means the interest rate on the loan will change as the prime rate or LIBOR changes.

The rate on a typical subprime loan will be the prime rate or LIBOR plus a specified interest rate. For example, if the prime rate is 6.5% a subprime loan might be 6.5% plus 5% for a total of 11.5%. If prime goes to 7% then the interest rate on an adjustable rate changes and the new rate would be 12%.

Many ARMs are tied to the LIBOR so if the prime rate goes down the interest rate on the LIBOR pegged loan might not decrease.

Here's the backward thing about the mortgage business. The people who are least able to pay are charged the most for the same loan amount to adjust for the increased risk.

It is the very fact that they are charged more that has contributed to the subprime mortgage crisis. For example, if you have a low credit score you may pay 10% interest for a loan that someone with a high credit score might get for 5% interest.

A $250,000 subprime loan paid over 30 years at 10% interest has monthly payments of $2,193 and total payments of $789,814.

In contrast, a $250,000 prime loan paid over 30 years at 5% interest has monthly payments of $1,342 and total payments of $483,138.

The person who can least afford the loan is paying $851 more per month (a 63.4% increase over prime) and an additional $306,676 in interest for the exact same amount of borrowed money, $250,000.

Chapter 2
The Role of Congress &
The Federal Reserve

"The nine most terrifying words in the English language are: 'I'm from the government and I'm here to help.'"
-Ronald Reagan

 Why would banks, the pillars of fiscal responsibility and risk aversion, lend money to people who couldn't afford to repay it? The short answer is, they wouldn't, and until thirty years ago they didn't. So what changed? The short answer is that Congress strongly encouraged and, in a sense, mandated it.

 Thirty years ago homebuyers who fell into today's subprime category would have been denied credit. Back then, many of our Congressional leaders thought this was discriminatory. Congress wanted to give everyone the opportunity to own his or her own home, even those who weren't creditworthy. They believed that much of the run-down housing in the inner city was the result of discrimination.

Here we are thirty years later and we still have the run-down housing in the inner city, but now we also have a subprime mortgage crisis. Mission accomplished? I don't think so.

Between 1975 and 1980 Congress passed four pieces of legislation that forced our financial institutions into the subprime market.

The first was The Home Mortgage Disclosure Act (HMDA), which required lending institutions to report their loan data. By 1977 this provided Congress with the information they needed to prove that lending institutions were discriminating against poor people by not providing them with loans.

> "The Home Mortgage Disclosure Act (HMDA), enacted by Congress in 1975 and implemented by the Federal Reserve Board's Regulation C, requires lending institutions to report public loan data (1)."

In 1977 Congress passed, and President Bill Clinton signed, The Community Reinvestment Act (CRA). This act requires lending institutions to provide loans to people in low and moderate income neighborhoods. There are stiff penalties for financial institutions that don't provide loans to low and moderate-income people.

> The CRA "is intended to encourage depository institutions to help meet the credit needs of the communities in which they operate, including low- and moderate-income

neighborhoods, consistent with safe and sound banking operations. It was enacted by the Congress in 1977 (12 U.S.C. 2901) and is implemented by Regulations 12 CFR parts 25, 228, 345, and 563e (2)."

Two things happened as a result of the CRA. First, banks closed branches in poor neighborhoods so they wouldn't have to loan money in those areas. Many have never returned. Second, they needed to find a way to charge higher rates and fees for loans to low and moderate-income earners. Financial institutions can't afford to make loans to low and moderate-income people without charging higher rates to compensate for a higher default rate.

The Depository Institutions Deregulatory and Monetary Control Act (DIDMCA) passed by Congress in 1980, eliminated restrictions on interest rates for home loans (among other things) that allowed financial institutions to charge borrowers a premium interest rate (3).

And in 1982 the Alternative Mortgage Transaction Parity Act (AMTPA) allowed lenders to charge variable interest rates and use balloon payments (4).

And thus it was that the subprime mortgage market was born. What's ironic is that some of the same congressional leaders who insisted our financial institutions lend to low-income people are now charging our financial institutions with 'predatory lending'.

It seems to me that it would be logical to question how lending institutions can provide loans to people who can't afford to repay them? The short answer is they can't. Apparently that wasn't a concern for Congress.

So what did financial institutions do? They sold the loans to someone else and thus the securitization of subprime mortgages was born (discussed later). Did our Congressional leaders really believe in their long term strategy with the HMDA, CRA, DIDMCA & AMTPA? Did our congressional leaders even think about the long term implications of their legislation? Do our congressional leaders understand their role in the subprime mess?

What about the Federal Reserve?

- Chairman Greenspan was a big supporter of ARMs in 2004. His rate increases over the next 24 months made those same ARMs unaffordable for most subprime borrowers.

- In 2005 he dismissed the idea of a housing bubble, saying it was a regional issue.

- In 2006 he suggested that we'd seen the bottom of the housing slump.

If you want to read more about the role of the Federal Reserve and Alan Greenspan's speeches here are some URL's for your reference.

http://www.federalreserve.gov/boarddocs/speeches/2003/20030304/default.htm

http://www.federalreserve.gov/newsevents/speech/2004speech.htm

http://www.federalreserve.gov/BOARDDOCS/TESTIMONY/2005/200506092/default.htm

www.access.gpo.gov/congress/senate/pdf/108hrg/86497.pdf

Subprime

I believe Greenspan's decision to hold interest rates low for so long was a major contributor to the current crisis. Greenspan held the fed funds rate at 1% for 12 months, from July 2003 to July 2004. How was this a contributor to the crisis? Because historically interest rates were much higher. For most of 1998 the rate was 5.5% and for most of 2000 the rate was 6.5%. By making it so cheap to borrow money for so long it gave people an opportunity to borrow much more money than they otherwise would have been able to afford.

Finally when the Federal Open Market Committee (FOMC) did start to raise rates in July 2004, they raised rates nearly every time they met, a total of 17 times. The fed funds rate went from 1% to 5.25%. People didn't have time to get out of the financial obligations they signed up for when the rates were 1%.

Let's suppose that you had a $200,000 subprime mortgage for a house that you bought in 2004. The rate on your mortgage started out at 2% but adjusted to prime plus 5% during the time that the FOMC raised the rates from 1% to 5.25%. What would your payments look like for a 30 year mortgage?

Amount of the Loan = $200,000

Payment at 2% = $739 / month

Payment at 10.25% (prime plus 5%) = $1,792/month

That's an increase of over $1,000 per month or 142%.

No wonder so many subprime borrowers are in trouble. The FOMC raised rates too quickly. The subprime borrowers didn't have time to refinance at more reasonable rates. You could've borrowed at 2% in 2004 and by the time your adjustable rate mortgage was set to adjust two years later your interest rate could've risen by 10% (4.25% for the increase in the prime rate plus the 5% for subprime).

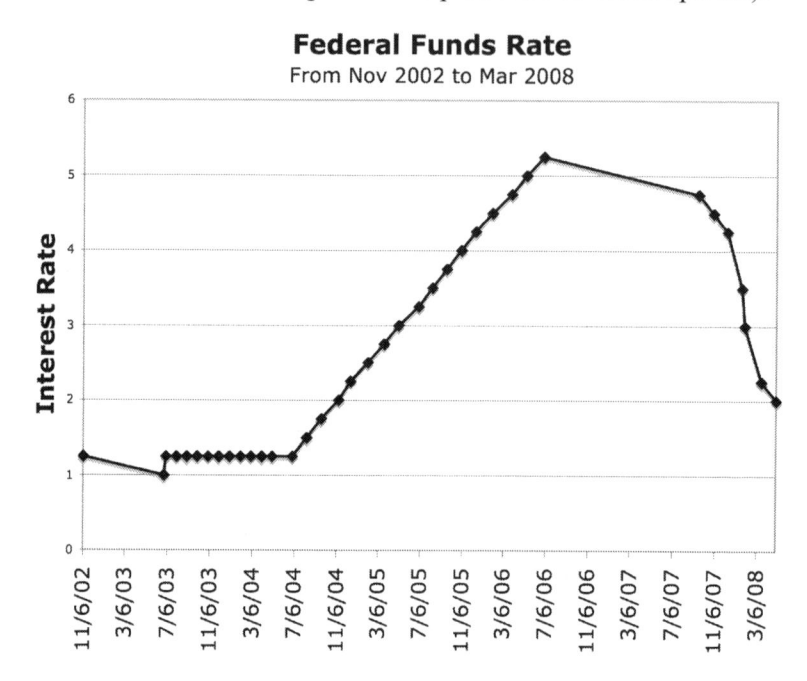

Federal Funds Rate
From Nov 2002 to Mar 2008

Source: federalreserve.gov (5)

    I believe that if the FOMC had raised rates more slowly the housing bubble would have deflated slowly and we wouldn't have the crisis we do today.

    Greenspan and the Federal Reserve had it so horribly wrong. It's interesting that so many people hold him in such high regard. Is it regard for the position or for the accomplishments?

    I am writing this book in June 2008. The Federal Reserve cut the fed funds rate down to 2% in May. The economy is slowing but not contracting, so technically we are not in a recession.

The May jobs report just came out and we lost 49,000 jobs. That was a little worse than expected. In April 2008 we only lost 20,000 jobs; the economists had expected as many as 75,000 jobs lost.

The Fed is cutting rates for several reasons:

- By making money less expensive to borrow they are stimulating the economy. Businesses can more easily afford to borrow money to invest and expand. They can afford to hire more people and purchase more business equipment.

- Consumers can more easily afford to borrow money to purchase goods and services. Consumer spending is a huge factor in the health of our economy.

- By dropping the fed funds rate the prime lending rate goes down as well. When the prime rate goes down the interest rate on many Adjustable Rate Mortgages goes down as well. That makes borrowers' mortgage payments more affordable which will help reduce foreclosures, which in turn will help improve the real estate market.

- Finally, by cutting interest rates the Fed hopes to reverse the trend of the contraction of available credit. The contraction of available credit goes far beyond homeowners and consumers. The contraction of credit has forced companies like the once proud Bear Stearns out of business along with hundreds of other financial services (mortgage, etc.) companies.

However, there is a cost to be paid for cutting interest rates. The value of the dollar goes down, down, down.

That is why I just paid $4 for a gallon of gas. As the value of our currency falls, goods and services become more expensive. Inflation!

The reason the government numbers for inflation look so tame is because they exclude energy and food. After housing, these are two of the biggest expenditures for the average American family. Excluding food and energy may make sense in an economic analysis but for practical purposes, regardless of what the government reports, we are experiencing inflation and it is painful.

Chapter 3
History Repeats Itself

"I'm living so far beyond my income that we may almost be said to be living apart."
-E. E. Cummings

This is not the first time we've experienced problems with subprime loans. Do you recall the demise of Long Term Capital Management (LTCM) in 1998? Perhaps not, so let me explain.

LTCM was a hedge fund founded in 1994 by the former head of bond trading at Salomon Brothers, a huge Wall Street investment bank. LTCM used leverage (borrowed money) to invest. They had almost $5 billion in capital, which sounds like a great deal of money until you learn that they were trading $1.25 trillion in derivative positions.

In order to be able to trade $1.25 trillion they had to have approximately 10% of the $1.25 trillion in their trading account or $125 billion, which they borrowed.

So let's examine their positions in terms of percentages. They had $5 billion in capital and had borrowed $125 billion. That's means they had 4% equity and 96% borrowed funds. But they traded ten times the amount of money they borrowed. If they experienced losses of ½% they were out of business. Actually, they were very smart people and for a long time, they made a lot of money. Annual returns of 50% weren't uncommon. Their trading strategy has been compared to picking up nickels in front of a steamroller. Unfortunately, in the end the steamroller won.

We had two major financial problems that came into play during that time period.

- First the Russians defaulted on their government bonds thereby devaluing their currency.

- Second was the Asian financial crisis.

Both of these events created an abrupt move away from risk in the financial markets.

The result was a massive contraction of available credit. In a highly volatile worldwide financial system LTCM hadn't made a good bet.

At first the losses, approximately $500 million, were manageable. But as the crisis worsened and the losses increased the LTCM investors decided they'd had enough and began to withdraw their money.

Before long LTCM was down to $600 million in capital (a 90% reduction). With the already huge leverage this made their exposure to risk even worse. They needed cash, and lots of it.

Because of the contraction of available credit, they were unable to borrow enough money. Although there were offers of a buyout, LTCM rejected them. Instead the Federal Reserve Bank of New York orchestrated a bailout.

This should sound familiar to those who read about Bear Stearns. After massive losses in the subprime market Bear Stearns needed billions of dollars of capital. They couldn't borrow the money because of the contraction in the credit markets and so agreed to a rescue plan orchestrated by the Federal Reserve (more on that later).

The contraction of available credit impacted more than just LTCM back in the late 90's. During that time period a half dozen of the largest subprime lenders also declared bankruptcy as a result of the contraction of available credit.

The 2007-2008 subprime crisis is also a direct result of the contraction of available credit. When investors could not accurately value the worth of subprime bonds they stopped buying them and available credit evaporated. This issue will be examined in detail later.

History was bound to repeat itself and this time is no exception. As long as the free market system has been around there have always been boom and bust business cycles. The real estate bubble was bound to burst sooner or later. Now that it has burst, let's look at some of the reasons why.

Chapter 4
Exploding ARMs

"But no, they're like, 'Oh, we're not gonna give you money unless you prove you don't need it! I mean, what kind of a system is that?"
-Willow Rosenberg (Buffy V.S.)

Why are there so many foreclosures? It isn't because of massive unemployment or a horrible recession (although the subprime mess may cause a recession). No, the answer is simply because too many people bought more than they could afford.

Before we dive into the details of the current financial crisis, let's look at the loan that I believe started this mess: the option Adjustable Rate Mortgage (option ARM), also known as the exploding ARM.

This loan has several options that can get a borrower in big financial trouble.

- One option provides for a very low introductory interest rate that adjusts to a higher rate after one to seven years.

- Another option allows the borrower to pay only the interest on the loan for a specified period of time and then the rate adjusts and the borrower must pay interest and start repaying the principal.

- Another option allows the borrower to pay less interest than what is due, with the balance added to the mortgage (negative amortization).

- There are many other variations to the option ARM.

Frequently option ARMs carry a pre-payment penalty. In other words, if you pay off your mortgage early <u>or if you refinance your loan</u> you'll have to pay a financial penalty. Sometimes these penalties can be very, very large.

Some option ARMs carry balloon payments in which the borrower will have to pay off the loan at the end of a specified period of time. For example, the loan payments may reflect a 40-year amortization but the total amount of the loan will be due in five or seven years. For example, a $185,000 loan with a 40-year amortization schedule would mean a monthly payment of $1,083. But at the end of the 5 or 7-year period you'd have to repay the $185,000 or get a new loan. Not a bad deal if:

- Interest rates don't go up.

- There isn't a big pre-payment penalty.

- You can afford a traditional 30-year mortgage payment; say 6.5%, which would mean a payment of around $1,250.

- You can refinance after five or seven years. Some reasons you may not be able to refinance include:
    - The bank is no longer loaning money in that particular neighborhood.
    - Some of your neighbors' homes have been foreclosed driving your property value down and now you don't have enough equity to qualify for a loan.
    - Your credit score has declined and you no longer qualify for a loan.
    - You've lost your job or don't have the income to qualify for a loan.

Let's take an in-depth look at an example. Suppose you wanted to buy a $200,000 home with a $15,000 down payment. At 6.5% interest for a 30-year loan, the finances of the purchase would look something like this:

House value: $200,000

Loan value: $185,000

Monthly Principal & Interest: $1,250

Monthly Property Tax & Insurance: $250

Total monthly payment = $1,500

Here's an example of the option ARM whereby the borrower pays less than the amount due on the loan. There are many variations on the option ARM but for right now let's examine the most basic. You owe $1,500 each month, but you can pay less than you owe. It varies but for this example let's say you can pay $1,000. The extra $500 per month is added to your principal. This is called negative amortization. So at the end of year one you'll owe $191,000 instead of $185,000. The extra $6,000 represents the $500 per month for 12 months.

Now here's where the exploding part of the ARM comes into play. Loans were made to borrowers with low introductory rates. For example, instead of paying 6.5% they could pay just 2.5% for the first 3 years and then it would adjust to a higher rate. Sometimes it adjusts to near credit card rates for the least creditworthy borrowers. That same $1,500 payment at 2.5% would allow you to afford a much larger mortgage. Add to that the ability to pay only part of what is owed and you can see how the payment on a mortgage like that could explode.

For example, suppose you want to buy a house and can afford $1,500 per month mortgage payment. You could use an option ARM mortgage with a 2.5% interest rate that will give you a mortgage payment of $1,500 (you could get a mortgage with a payment of $2,500 due but you only have to pay $1,500 because negative amortization of $1,000 yields an actual payment of $1,500). Remember the true value of that mortgage is $2,500 per month even though you're only paying $1,500 at the beginning of the loan.

So how much house does that buy? I think you'll be amazed to find that you can get a $625,000 loan for $2,500 per month at 2.5% interest.

But what happens when that mortgage rate adjusts and the bank no longer allows negative amortization. Here are the payments for a $625,000 loan at several interest rates.

- At 6.5% the payment is $3,950 – EXPLOSION

- At 8.5% the payment is $4,800 – EXPLOSION

- At 10.5% the payment is $5,700 - EXPLOSION

Most borrowers will probably have their first adjustment to the 8.5% range, but remember this is an adjustable rate mortgage. As the Federal Reserve raises interest rates the mortgage rate climbs, so 10.5% could be right around the corner. Borrowers who have had credit problems will find their rates adjust much, much higher than 10.5%.

So this borrower started out with a payment of $1,500 and now has a payment of $4,800 at 8.5%. That's an increase of 220%. Obviously this mortgage isn't affordable for this borrower but the sad truth is that many people were lead to believe they could afford this type of loan – the exploding ARM.

This is just one example. There are many variations on the exploding ARM.

Here's another example. Suppose a borrower bought a $200,000 house with a $185,000 mortgage that started out at 6.5% without negative amortization. Their mortgage payment was $1,250. For many homeowners in this situation, when their rates adjusted they went to 10% or 12%. At 10% their new payment was $1,625 per month, an increase of almost $400 per month, an increase of over 30%. For homeowners where the $1,250 per month was a stretch, there is no way they could afford an extra $400 per month.

Or perhaps they had a $185,000 mortgage at 2.5% that adjusted to 8.5% after 2 years. At 2.5% their mortgage payment was $730 per month. At 8.5% their payment was $1422 per month, almost double.

It is important to note that the exploding ARM isn't just for the subprime market. Many prime borrowers selected this type of loan because it got them a bigger house with lower initial payments.

Why would the lender and mortgage broker provide people with this type of loan?

The answer is money, money, money, money and more money. The financial institutions and mortgage brokers made huge fees and commissions from these types of loans. Once the loans were completed the financial institutions sold the loans and they no longer carried the risk. The only incentive the mortgage broker had was to steer the borrower to the loan that provided the broker with the biggest commission. So whose best interests does the mortgage broker have in mind?

I'm not suggesting that all mortgage brokers are going to push borrowers to the loans where they make the most money, but follow the money and you'll see that is exactly what many mortgage brokers did.

This is an example of how greed drove the mortgage industry.

Chapter 5
Evolution of the Mortgage Business, Securitization and CDO's

"In the old days, it was the banks that originated loans and kept the loans. But once you went to securitization you created the possibility of the originator having different information from the buyer. Not only is there information asymmetry but in this context, there are perverse incentives. The originator has an incentive to provide distorted information. The buyers should have been aware of this, but it's quite apparent that they weren't as aware of this as they should have been."

-Joe Stiglitz

Ok so we have exploding ARMs and those people who bought more house than they should have are going to be foreclosed. How does that translate into a liquidity crisis with hundreds of billions of dollars in write-downs? To comprehend the financial crisis of 2007 and 2008 requires a little understanding of how the mortgage market works.

When financial institutions loan money to borrowers for mortgages, the financial institutions typically don't keep the mortgage. Instead the mortgages are packaged up and sold in the financial market so that the financial institutions that loaned the money can make another mortgage loan. The process of packaging and selling these mortgages is called securitization.

There are a couple of terms that the industry uses to describe this process. The packages of mortgages are called collateralized debt obligations (CDO's). Typically a CDO contains thousands of loans. CDO's can be backed by a variety of assets – homes, cars, equipment etc. When housing backs CDO's they are called mortgage-backed securities (MBS).

Before the Congressional legislation of the '70s that required financial institutions to loan money to low and moderate-income borrowers, most financial institutions would make mortgage loans and hold onto them until maturity or they were paid off. In those days, the financial institutions had an incentive to be certain the people they loaned money to could repay it. The loan officer would meet with the borrower and get to know them. They would find out about their job, how long they'd worked there, how much money they made, etc. The advent of mortgage-backed securities removed the incentive for financial institutions to be certain loans would be repaid and gave them access to virtually unlimited amounts of capital.

When financial institutions were required to loan money to those high-risk borrowers who in all likelihood would have difficulty repaying the loan, the financial institution needed to get those loans off their books by selling them to someone else. So they bundled them up and worked with credit rating agencies to determine the overall level of risk associated with a bundle of mortgages and sold them as bonds.

Financial institutions figured out how to sell their subprime loans many years ago and the growth of the subprime market skyrocketed. Not only does the financial institution make money from the borrowers' fees at the closing but they also make a profit when they sell the loans through securitization because they make a slice of the future interest to be paid. These days most of the mortgages are packaged up and sold in the bond market so that financial institutions can go through the process again and again...

What's interesting is that Congress, because of their legislation, and the Office of the Comptroller of the Currency, because of their lack of oversight, have created an entire industry that preys on the subprime borrower. Subprime borrowers are almost always forced to refinance to avoid the higher interest rates. Why would the financial industry want that? It's simple: money. They make a ton of money from the fees.

Securitization is also a very profitable business. The average CDO such as a mortgage-backed security is $1 billion. A typical investment bank will earn 1% to 1.5% on a CDO. That equals $15 million in fees on one CDO.

There are currently approximately $7 trillion in mortgage-backed securities, which equals approximately $70 to $100 billion in fees. That's a lot of fees. But wait, it gets better.

The original mortgage-backed securities can be sliced and diced again and again and again. Each time they are sliced and diced there are more fees. This was truly a money machine.

The people who provide the services associated with the fees earn their living from mortgage closings. The more closings they have, the more they get paid. Everyone involved has the incentive to do more closings whether or not the borrower can repay the loan.

Thus, Congress gave everyone involved in the mortgage market an incentive to make borrowers refinance their loans. So, it was only a matter of time before the loans were structured such that the borrowers would have no choice but to refinance.

The mortgage business has evolved so that the mortgage-originating financial institutions are now mainly only conduits to the money. The vast majority of all mortgages in the U.S. are securitized.

- 2007 annual mortgage volume = $2.5 trillion

- 2007 annual securitization of mortgages = $2 trillion

As part of the process of securitization the CDO's are given a credit rating by a credit rating agency. The credit rating agencies usually work closely with the financial institutions to try to represent the risk of the investment fairly and accurately. Theoretically, everyone should be able to understand the risks associated with these types of securities.

So who buys these CDO's? They are purchased by a wide variety of investors – institutional investors, hedge funds, mutual funds, investment banks, pension funds, etc. The list of investors goes on and on and includes virtually every country in the world. Not only did the world buy CDO's from the United States, but virtually every major industrialized nation also had their own financial institutions create and sell their own CDO's.

Securitization is a complex business. It would be easy to understand if it was simply packaging the mortgages and selling them, but it is far more complex.

For example, the interest can be sold separately from the principal. The mortgages can be pooled based upon the creditworthiness. The pools of mortgages can be broken up according to various risk/return profiles. A single pool may be broken up into a dozen different risk categories from high risk for high return to low risk for a prime rate return. There are a wide variety of combinations and derivatives.

As a result, it makes it difficult to determine the actual value of the mortgage-backed securities. Additionally, it can be difficult to determine who actually owns the right to the underlying asset, the house.

When word of U.S. subprime defaults began to hit the markets, financial institutions wanted to know the extent of their exposure. It proved difficult to determine the level of exposure for two reasons.

First, the mortgages were grouped together into large financial packages. So, it would be nearly impossible to determine the possibility of default because of the volume of mortgages in a single CDO.

Second, the bundle of mortgages can be sliced up so many different ways it is difficult to know who owns what. For example here are just some of the ways they can be sliced and diced.

Here are just a few ways to create a CDO

- Only the interest payments of all the loans.
- Only the principal payments of all the loans.
- Only the interest portion of the high-risk portion of the mortgages.
- Only the principal portion of the high-risk portion of the mortgages.
- Only the interest portion of the prime rate portion of the mortgages.
- Only the principal portion of the prime rate portion of the mortgages.
- Only the ARM portion of the mortgages.
- Only the interest portion of the ARM portion of the mortgages.
- Only the principal portion of the ARM portion of the mortgages.
- Only the interest portion of the high-risk portion (low credit score) of the ARM portion of the mortgages.
- Only the insured portion of loans.
- Only the uninsured portion of the loans.
- Any combination of the above and many more.

As you can see CDO's can be apportioned many different ways. We also have derivatives to take into account. Needless to say the topic is complex and it is difficult to value these securities after they've been sliced and diced and perhaps re-sliced and re-diced.

Investors don't like uncertainty. In the fall of 2007, when investors couldn't determine their level of exposure to risk in the subprime market, they did three things.

- First, they decided to stop purchasing the CDO's.

- Second, they decided to sell any CDO's they owned that might have exposure to the subprime market. As CDO's flooded the market their prices began to fall dramatically. How far will the value of CDO's fall? Only time will tell.

- Third, if they were lending institutions, they raised their interest rates on loans in an effort to hang onto their remaining cash. The increases in interest rates impacted every loan category from mortgages to car loans to inter-bank lending to lines of credit.

The impact was felt on many fronts.

- First, the value of CDO's fell by 30% in the first couple of months, and I wouldn't be surprised to see CDO's sell for 20 cents on the dollar before it's all over.

- Investors who had borrowed money to purchase CDO's, primarily hedge funds, needed additional cash to shore up their now shaky financial position because of the decline in the value of the CDO's they held.

- It is important to understand that some hedge funds leveraged their investments by borrowing enormous amounts of money to purchase CDO's (remember LTCM). When the value of the CDO's began to decline it quickly depleted any available cash. They needed to borrow cash, lots of it and quickly, for three main reasons. First, they needed to make their loan payments. Second, they needed to maintain their 10% ratio of equity to investment portfolio. Third, customers were withdrawing funds and they needed cash to be able to redeem the customer requests. This demand for cash was enormous, putting further strain on an already stressed financial system. If cash wasn't available, investors were forced to sell their CDO's to cover their loan payments. Because it was difficult to sell the CDO's, investors had to dramatically discount the CDO's to sell them and raise the cash they needed. The net effect was to further drive down the value of the CDO's.

- Suddenly the mortgage-originating financial institutions weren't able to profitably sell their CDO's to raise money to lend money to borrowers for new mortgages. Mortgages became increasingly difficult to get, even for borrowers with good credit.

- Large numbers of subprime lenders began going out of business.

- Because of rising interest rates, adjustable rate mortgages went that much higher and the rates on new mortgages also went up. Money was more expensive because no one wanted to lend – financial institutions wanted to discourage borrowing by increasing their interest rates. They thought they might need the money to shore up their own finances since they didn't know the extent of their exposure to the subprime market.

- Business deals that were previously profitable at a lower interest rate suddenly became unprofitable at higher interest rates and as a result the deals didn't get done.

- Banking customers in some parts of the world began to panic and withdraw their funds. This further strained the liquidity of the financial system by removing available cash.

Financial institutions did have some insurance. There are insurance companies and re-insurance companies that would guarantee the value of the CDO's. The key words here are 'some insurance'. Not all CDO's had insurance against default and those that did have insurance were not always fully insured. Those that were fully insured might bankrupt the insurance company if they were to collect all the insurance that has been written.

What about Private Mortgage Insurance (PMI)? Many borrowers who didn't have a 20% down payment had to pay for PMI as part of their mortgage payment. The same companies that insured the CDO's insured the individual mortgages and they don't have enough cash reserves to cover all the losses.

In other words, there is protection but not enough for the entire market. Regarding the question of whether the company providing the insurance had the assets to provide the extraordinary amount of money they'll need in the event of massive defaults: my guess is they didn't. When they try to raise the capital they'll find it difficult if not impossible so we'll see bond re-insurance companies go out of business as well.

What started out as prudent business practices in the subprime market gradually eroded into the situation we have today. At first only a few institutions were making subprime loans. When others saw the easy money they jumped on the bandwagon. Before you know it we've got an entire industry catering to subprime borrowers. There was big, big money involved. No one wanted to let their competitor get ahead of them in the subprime business.

I heard a story about an Emergency Medical Technician who qualified for a million dollar home. Sound outrageous? Here's how it happened. She went to a mortgage broker who didn't require income verification who found a bank that didn't require income verification. She said she her annual salary was $300,000 and so she qualified for the loan. Her actual salary was around $60,000 per year. Of course, she couldn't afford the payments and because of the contraction of available credit she couldn't refinance the home and was foreclosed.

She could've kept the home if:

- The value of the home continued to increase.

- She was able to refinance.

- The increased value was enough to provide her with cash back when she refinanced.

- She used the cash back to pay the mortgage.

That's a lot of 'ifs'.

Securitization changed the rules of the mortgage business. It essentially provided unlimited liquidity to financial institutions for mortgages. As a result there were many loans that never should have been underwritten.

Chapter 6
The Magic of Wall Street

"October: This is one of the particularly dangerous months to invest in stocks. Other dangerous months are July, January, September, April, November, May, March, June, December, August and February."

-Mark Twain

I've always thought a picture is worth a thousand words. So in this chapter I show how the money flows from the borrower through Wall Street and out to the ultimate lenders.

(1) A nurse wants to buy a house, but doesn't qualify for a prime loan so she goes to a mortgage broker

(2) The **mortgage broker** calls around and finds a loan from a bank that will accept a subprime customer and pays the biggest commission.

(3) The Broker fills out the mortgage application paperwork

(4) Bank approves the loan

(5) Nurse signs the paperwork at closing, gets a mortgage & buys the house

(5a) Bank pays Broker $$$$ Commission

(6) When the **bank** has enough mortgage loans they will bundle them together & sell them to Wall Street.

Mortgage Paperwork

$$$$

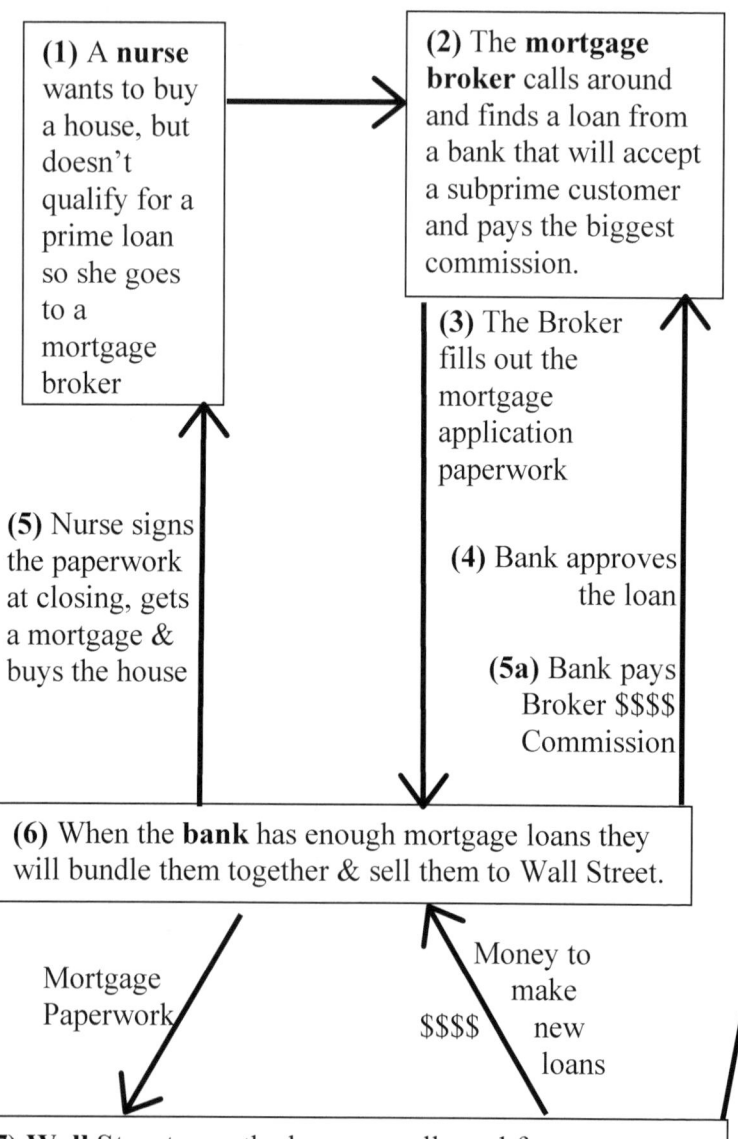

Money to make new loans

(7) Wall Street uses the loans as collateral for a new security. They call these securities CDO (collateralized debt obligations) and MBS (mortgage backed securities). But who will be dumb enough to buy mortgages made to people who couldn't afford to make the payments?

Subprime _____ Page 45

(8) Here's where the magic happens. The Wall Street firm breaks up the loans into risk groups – for example - Good, Bad & Ugly. They pay prime interest rate on the Good loans and get insurance on those loans so they get a AAA rating (the best rating means virtually no risk). The bad loans will get a BBB rating and pay a premium over prime because of the increased risk. They won't even bother trying to sell the Ugly loans. Instead they'll setup a corporation and sell the Ugly loans to their own dummy corporation. They call it a SPV, Special Purpose Vehicle. All the risk is moved to the SPV and doesn't show up on the Wall Street firm's books.

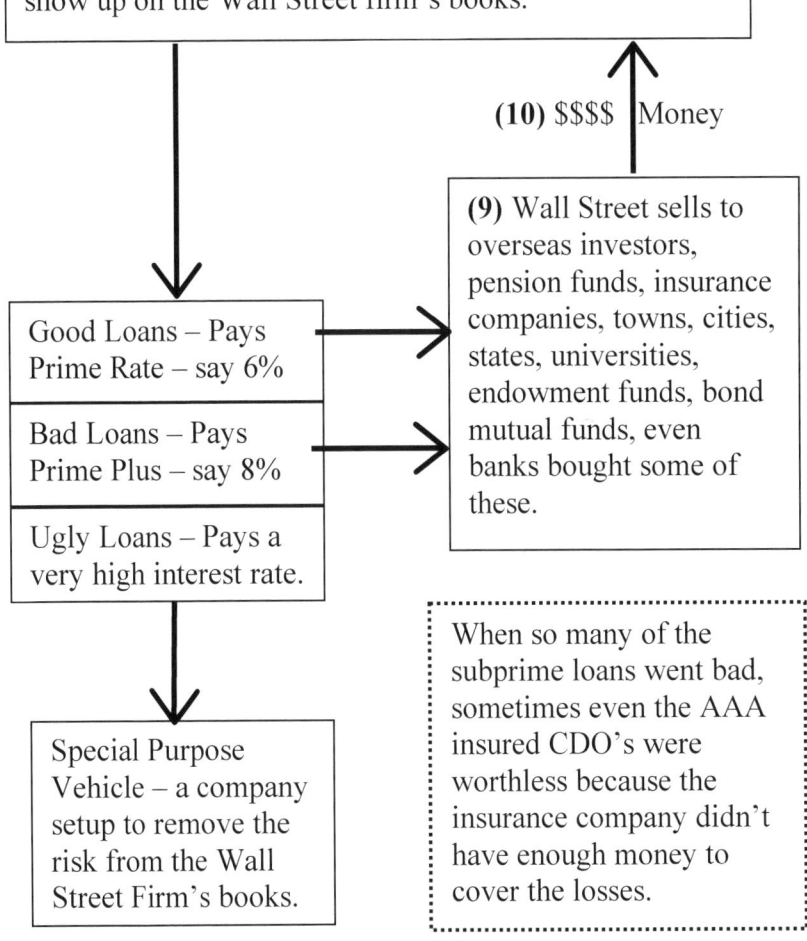

(10) $$$$ Money

(9) Wall Street sells to overseas investors, pension funds, insurance companies, towns, cities, states, universities, endowment funds, bond mutual funds, even banks bought some of these.

Good Loans – Pays Prime Rate – say 6%

Bad Loans – Pays Prime Plus – say 8%

Ugly Loans – Pays a very high interest rate.

Special Purpose Vehicle – a company setup to remove the risk from the Wall Street Firm's books.

When so many of the subprime loans went bad, sometimes even the AAA insured CDO's were worthless because the insurance company didn't have enough money to cover the losses.

Chapter 7
Scope of the Problem

"If you would know the value of money try to borrow some."
-Benjamin Franklin

    I don't want to bore you with endless statistics and references but I think it is important to understand the scope of the problem. So I will try to put the scope of the problem in perspective.

    I pulled numbers from a variety of government sources:

- The U.S. Federal Reserve

- The U.S. Census Bureau

- The U.S. Department of Commerce

- The U.S. Office of Policy Development & Research

- The Department of Housing and Urban Development.

All these numbers have been rounded, in some cases to the nearest trillion dollars. Wouldn't you like to be able to round your finances to the nearest trillion?

Today there are approximately $7 trillion in mortgage-backed securities that have been packaged up and sold on Wall Street. Everyone who bought subprime mortgage-backed bonds lost money. But it isn't just the buyers. Remember that Wall Street firms didn't get rid of the 'ugly' bonds; they just moved them into offshore SPV's so they wouldn't show up on their balance sheets and have a negative impact on their stock price, <u>but they still own them</u>.

That's why you saw Bear Stearns, one of the world's largest global investment banks; require an emergency rescue package on March 18, 2008 by JP Morgan. Bear Stearns, the high flying company founded in 1923 whose stock once sold for over $100 per share, agreed to be acquired for $2 per share which was later increased to $10. Now that's ugly.

It's not just ugly for Bear Stearns and bondholders; some of the CDO's had repurchase agreements. Should defaults exceed pre-determined percentages financial institutions will be obligated to buy back the CDO's that are now worthless. Now that's really ugly.

Back to the $7 trillion in mortgage backed securities. To put that in perspective, the GDP is $14 trillion (GDP stands for Gross Domestic Product and is the sum of all good and services sold in the U.S.). That means mortgage-backed securities are worth roughly 50% of one year's GDP. That's a very large number!

However, we need to put it in perspective of our total net worth. U.S. households have approximately $60 trillion in net worth (assets minus liabilities). So while there is $7 trillion in mortgage-backed securities that represents only about 10% of our net worth.

Ok, so there is a huge dollar value of mortgage-back securities. How many of those are delinquent? According to the Census Bureau there are about 80 million homes in the US and about 50 million of those have mortgages (6). There are a wide variety of estimates and numbers floating around but the estimates I've heard most frequently quoted from government surveys are that 2 million households are in foreclosure and 5 million mortgages are delinquent.

OK, that's bad, but it's not the end of the world.

How has the subprime problem impacted the overall U.S. housing market? In 2006 there were about 8.5 million homes sold. In 2007 there were about 5.5 million homes to be sold. That's a reduction of about 35%. A 35% reduction is a huge number in any business. When you're talking about the real estate business, where the transaction value runs in the hundreds of thousands, a reduction of this magnitude boggles the mind.

At the beginning of 2008 there were about 4 million homes for sale, which translates into almost one year's worth of inventory. That is the most inventory we've had since the '80s. With that many homes on the market it is going to take a while to work down the excess inventory. The law of supply and demand predicts that while we have too much inventory prices can only go down.

The peak value of the U.S. housing stock was over $20 trillion by the middle of 2006. The loss of value in housing is 16% or $3.2 trillion as of June 2008. Some estimates have that growing to $5 trillion by the end of 2008. That's just the loss of value in the housing stock.

That $5 trillion loss doesn't include the loss of jobs in many housing related industries: the construction business, the mortgage closing business (brokers, processors, appraisers, title search & insurance, lawyers etc.), the financial services sector (brokers, banks, etc.), the suppliers to the home building business (concrete, lumber, drywall, electrical fixtures, plumbing, HVAC, roofing, insulation, siding, windows, doors, flooring, granite, appliances, home furnishings, etc.). The loss could be much, much larger and the recession much, much worse.

This is not just a U.S. problem. One of the positive things about mortgage-backed securities is the ability to spread the risk. People and institutions from all over the world bought these types of bonds.

Because our financial institutions were able to spread the risk they were able to make more loans thereby providing more people with the opportunity to own a home. In 2007 70% of all households owned their own home (or at least they thought they did, since most people had a mortgage, really the bank owned the home).

Many of these U.S. mortgage backed securities wound up being owned by overseas investors. Those investors are at risk now because of defaults on the loans behind the mortgage-backed securities. Additionally, many countries had subprime loans of their own that were in turn collateralized and turned into mortgage-backed securities.

Ok, so this is a worldwide problem. How does the U.S. stack up against other countries as far as the financial risk? There are two parts to this problem.

- First is the exposure of our financial systems to the contraction of credit and losses in the mortgage-backed securities. In that regard we are seriously exposed. Most of the mortgage-backed securities were sold to U.S. firms. The contraction of credit will impact virtually every business in the U.S.

- Second is the impact on the value of our housing stock and the overall setback in the business of building and selling houses as well as all of the industries that supply the home building business. In this regard we are also seriously exposed.

There is another area of concern, Fannie Mae and Freddie Mac. The Federal National Mortgage Association (Fannie Mae) is a 'government sponsored enterprise' but it is still a shareholder owned corporation with no government guarantee for the mortgages they back. The Federal Home Loan Mortgage Corporation (Freddie Mac) is also a 'government sponsored enterprise' and it is also a shareholder owned corporation with no government guarantee for the mortgage-backed securities they sell on the open market.

Some people in our government have suggested that the U.S. treasury provide a guarantee for all Freddie Mac & Fannie Mae securities. Judging by the scope of the problem, having Fannie & Freddie backed by the treasury could quickly bankrupt U.S. government.

So how did we get ourselves into this situation?

Chapter 8
Why Subprime?

"One of the strange things about life is that the poor, who need money the most, are the very ones that never have it."
-Finley Peter Dunne

The first question that comes to mind is why did our financial institutions make subprime loans? There are two answers to that question.

- The first answer is profit.

- The second answer is that the government forced them to make subprime loans.

Thirty years ago subprime borrowers were basically out of luck. They couldn't get a loan. The government felt that these subprime borrowers were being discriminated against.

In reality the banks didn't want to loan them money because they were high risk and many of them wouldn't be able to repay the loan.

Nevertheless, the government stepped in (through the CRA etc.) and insisted that our financial institutions loan money to subprime borrowers. Since banks and financial institutions that originate mortgages are not in the business to lose money they had to find some way of getting rid of those subprime loans.

So financial institutions came up with a solution. They would lend money to subprime borrowers, then sell the loan for a profit through securitization and do it all again and again as many times as they can. The more they repeat the process the more money they make.

With almost 25% of all Americans falling into the subprime category there is a huge market for subprime loans. Even people that didn't need a subprime loan, because they qualified for a prime loan, sometimes used a subprime loan.

How does someone end up being a subprime customer? It's easier than you might think. Here are some of the reasons:

- No documentation – there are a variety of reasons for this – failure to file tax returns, self-employment, illegal aliens, poor record keeping

- No credit score – relatively new to the job market or no previous credit – some people don't like credit cards and they don't borrow money

- Low credit score – less than 620 out of 850

- Late loan payments – it only takes two payments 60 days late or one that is 90 days late

- Non-payment of a loan – if a judgment has been entered

- Previous financial problems – bankruptcy, foreclosure, repossession, etc.

Subprime loans, current bad press aside, do have a place in the market.

Some borrowers, who qualified for a prime loan, chose a subprime loan so that they could use the low introductory interest rate to buy a bigger home.

Subprime loans have helped many people purchase homes that otherwise wouldn't have access to the credit markets. Subprime loans have also helped people establish or re-establish their credit. When someone defaults on a loan it is very difficult to get another loan. If they want to buy something on credit they have to start somewhere and that's where a subprime lender can provide a valuable service.

That's the good news.

The bad news is that because loaning money to low and moderate-income borrowers carries higher risk it also carries higher costs. Those costs are paid by those least able to afford it – the low and moderate-income borrower. Along with the necessity of charging higher fees to offset the higher costs comes the potential for abuse. Mortgage brokers have steered millions of borrowers to higher cost loans because of higher commissions. In fact, mortgage brokers have even steered prime borrowers to subprime loans because of the higher commissions.

There are many other types of subprime loans besides mortgages. For example, there are subprime loans for cars, credit cards, furniture etc. Some of the worst examples of abuse of subprime lending have come from a few credit card companies.

I don't want to put all subprime credit card lenders in a negative light, but some subprime credit cards can be financially brutal. I've heard stories where the fees to activate the card completely consume the available credit.

Here's how. Let's say someone gets one of these $150 credit cards for subprime borrowers.

- There's a $49.95 application fee.

- There's a $49.95 credit check fee.

- There's a $49.95 card activation fee.

Look at that, you have 15 cents of available credit, which makes it easy to max it out. The rates on these cards are as high as legally possible within the usury limits, usually 29.99%. Ouch! Imagine paying $150 to get 15 cents credit.

If you charge $1 for a cup of coffee you could be socked with a $50 over the credit limit fee.

Some credit cards don't offer a grace period, which results in late fees (if the customer isn't over the limit but is close to their credit limit, the late fee can push them over the limit, which results in over-the-limit fees.)

If you are a day late you might be charged a $50 late fee. Oops, the check bounced, now there's a $50 bad check fee.

You can see why it would be easy to max out the credit limit for a card like this.

You've purchased $1 with your credit card but you owe $350 at 29% interest – which equates to roughly $100 interest per year for a $1 purchase. This is bad for the consumer, but great business for the credit card company. Some call it predatory lending.

When does a subprime mortgage loan work?

- When the borrower can make the loan payments – both now, and if they have an ARM, after the loan adjusts to a higher rate.

- The borrower doesn't count on appreciating property values to bail them out. When housing is appreciating, it certainly makes refinancing out of a higher cost loan easier, but the borrower still needs to watch out for pre-payment penalties.

- When the borrower has adequate savings after purchasing the home. A good rule of thumb is six months living expenses.

- When the borrower has fully documented their income.

Who should use a subprime loan?

I believe only those who don't qualify for a prime loan should use a subprime loan because of the extra costs and fees associated with subprime loans. Some of the additional costs associated with subprime loans include: higher points, additional up front costs, mortgage broker commissions and pre-payment penalties.

Of all these extra costs the pre-payment penalty is probably the most damaging to the subprime borrower. At times the pre-payment penalty is so large it prevents the borrower from refinancing. Why? Because either the borrower doesn't have enough cash to pay the pre-payment penalty or they don't have enough equity in their home to roll the pre-payment penalty back into the mortgage. Their choice is to either make the higher mortgage payment when the rate adjusts or to sell the house.

The pre-payment penalty is how the lender is able to pay the broker a commission (often hidden and disguised as a yield spread premium), because the financial institution knows they'll get their money back when the loan is refinanced and they get their pre-payment penalty. *The commission the lender pays to the broker is in addition to the commission the borrower is paying.*

Chapter 9
Victims and Losers

"It's amazing how fast later comes when you buy now!"
-Milton Berle

So who are the victims and losers?

It's not just the subprime customers who are getting hurt. It's all of us. Barney Frank is proposing a bill that would allow banks to dump bad loans on the FHA. Guess who is going to pay for that. You are with your taxes.

For most of us that don't have a subprime mortgage we might think this is someone else's problem. But the sad truth is that even if we aren't planning on selling our homes in the near future, our homes have lost value that will take years to recover.

But the pain doesn't stop there. 100 million U.S. residents have money in mutual funds and other Wall Street investments that will be negatively impacted by this situation. Even worse, if the government does a bailout we'll be paying for it for a long, long time into the future with more tax dollars.

If your mortgage company has gone out of business, and there are hundreds of mortgage companies that have gone out of business, you'll receive a notice in the mail that someone else is servicing your mortgage. Beware of a couple of things.

- First, if your previous mortgage company escrowed your insurance and property taxes you need to contact your insurance company and your county tax collector to be certain those were paid. It has happened where a company servicing mortgages has gone out of business and did not pay the taxes and insurance. Good luck getting your money back if this happens to you.

- Second, you need to make sure that your escrow balance was transferred correctly. It is highly possible the new servicing agent won't credit your most recent payment. You should check on this second point any time your mortgage it switched to a new servicing agent, not just in the case of the servicing agent going out of business. You can verify your amortization schedule using one of the many tools available on the Internet.

There are other victims. For those who have purchased a home in the last few years they may see the value of their entire down payment disappear because of the decline in the value of their home. For many, this will represent their life savings. Heaven forbid they have to move in the next year, the house might not even be worth what they paid for it. How would you like to put $30,000 down (20%) on a

$150,000 house and a year later find your house is now only worth $110,000. You just lost $40,000. What a horrible situation but unfortunately one that many people who aren't subprime borrowers are finding themselves in.

Here's the worst part. Suppose they are foreclosed, they still owe the money or they may owe taxes on any debt that was forgiven.

How about the town where 2.5% of the housing stock is in foreclosure, or how about the condo development where half of the units are in foreclosure, for anyone who has their home for sale in one of those situations they are going to have to practically give it away.

In the case of the 50% empty condo development, the assessments are sure to increase because condos run on a tight budget and they need close to 100% occupancy to balance their budget. Routine maintenance and repairs still need to be taken care of while anything that isn't completely necessary will have to be deferred until occupancy returns to somewhere closer to 100%.

I'm sure you know or live close to someone who has had his or her house foreclosed. Take a look at any of the foreclosure websites. They live in your neighborhood. Listen to the radio and you'll hear ads for foreclosed homes. It's everywhere in the US.

I've also heard about people who've lost all the equity in their home, not hard to do if they only put 5% or 10% down. Some of these people are planning on walking away from their current home and defaulting on the mortgage but not until they've bought a comparable home nearby for much less than they owe on their current home. Think about it. Suppose they purchased a $300,000 home last year with 5% down and the market value of their home has declined by 20%. They've lost the $15,000 down payment and another $45,000. Instead of waiting for the market to turn around they are buying the same type of home they are in now for $240,000 and defaulting on their current mortgage once the sale of their new home goes through.

True, they'll have a default on their credit report but that is only after they've gotten their new mortgage. If they plan on living in the home for 7 years it will probably be off their report by then.

It's not just homeowners who are victims. Anyone who wants to borrow money is going to find it more difficult, for example, municipalities trying to issue their municipal bonds used to build infrastructure. That is a completely unrelated market that will be negatively impacted by the subprime problem.

Other categories of victims are homebuilders and their customers. I've heard of large condo projects that had been 75% pre-sold go out of business before any of the units had been completed.

Imagine putting a deposit down on a condo and selling your current home expecting to move into a completed project only to find out the builder has declared bankruptcy and your condo may never be finished and you may never get your deposit back.

This subprime mess can also impact people who've already moved into their new home. If the builder is bankrupt who will provide the warranty for the home? Or the homeowners may find there are liens on their home because the builder didn't pay the subcontractors.

Regardless of the type of home, there are many homebuilders who are in trouble because of the liquidity crisis. When a builder goes bankrupt it can impact an entire neighborhood leaving health clubs unfinished, unfinished golf courses, unpaved roads, clubhouses not built, unfinished homes and empty promises for community swimming pools. If the builder still owns property in the development it can also mean uncollected homeowners association dues, which puts an additional financial burden on the remaining homeowners.

Entire communities can be negatively impacted when residential construction is one of the largest employers in the area. When builders aren't building houses the carpenters, bricklayers, roofers, etc. are all out of work and at risk of losing their own home, possibly adding more foreclosure properties to a market already saturated with homes for sale.

So are there any winners in the subprime mess?

- Contrary to the rhetoric from politicians, it wasn't the financial institutions on Wall Street – they've had to write down hundreds of billions of dollars. Some have gone out of business. Those that remain may still be on the hook for the CDO's they've sold because of guarantees that defaults wouldn't exceed certain percentages.

- It wasn't the subprime mortgage lenders – many of them are out of business.

- It wasn't the investors– they've also lost billions on their investments.

There are a few winners.

- There were some hedge funds that bet the housing bubble would burst. They made money. But there were very few who made money this way.

- The CEO's and high level executives at many financial institutions made large salaries and bonuses. However, many of those same people are now out of work.

- Homebuyers who are just now entering the market for the first time may be winners. They will definitely pay less for a home than they would have in 2006, if they can get a mortgage. Because of the credit crisis mortgages are getting harder to come by. Also, if the value of homes continues to fall, it could wipe out their down payment and they'll move from the winner's column to the loser's column.

- Companies like Habitat for Humanity will find it easier to acquire land and may purchase extra land for future use while prices are depressed.

- Real estate investors with cash to buy properties are going to get some excellent bargains.

- Lastly, mortgage brokers are winners.

Of all the possible winners, I believe the biggest winners were the mortgage brokers. They made their money on the transaction with no vested interest in the mortgage other than commissions.

Don't get me wrong, Wall Street and our financial institutions made billions in fees, but if they ended up laid off, closing or selling their business, were they really winners?

I was listening to a news report on the radio about a gentleman who was behind in his payments on his subprime loans. It turns out he was a mortgage broker making $30,000 per month at the height of the subprime loan frenzy. That's right, $30,000 per month.

He had purchased a home for himself, his mother and an investment property with the same subprime loans he was offering to his customers. As the subprime market collapsed so did his job. Now he's unable to make his payments.

- To buy 3 homes, this gentleman must have thought he was going to make that kind of money for the rest of his life.

- Personally, I think it is outrageous for someone to make $30,000 per month as a mortgage broker. No special training. No higher education. You don't even need a high school diploma to be a mortgage broker. That's not to say that some people without a high school diploma don't work hard and earn $30,000 per month and earn every penny. I'm sure there are those who do. However, filling out paperwork for ignorant borrowers doesn't fall into that category in my opinion.

- The President of the United States only makes $33,333 per month.

- Even people who are in the mortgage business don't know how detrimental these types of loans can be if things don't go just right or they've come to believe their own marketing messages.

Most mortgage brokers work on commission, and their commission makes up the vast majority of their compensation. Their incentive is to make lots and lots of loans and to steer those loans to the financial institutions that pay the highest commission.

Everyone wants to know why so many loans were made to people who couldn't afford them. The simple answer is, because that's where the money is. Yes, the mortgage brokers were the biggest winners in the subprime mess. The broker with 3 mortgages is an example of greed, stupidity, ignorance and arrogance.

I'm sure many people would like to know if racial discrimination was involved in making subprime loans?

If that question were asked 30 years ago the answer would have been yes. However, for the most part, today the answer to this question is no.

According to a 2007 Federal Reserve study only about 2% of the 8,000+ lending institutions involved in the survey were found to have statistical differences in loans between whites and non-whites. Non-whites were more likely to acquire a subprime loan even when they didn't need to.

Were minorities specifically targeted for these loans because they were minorities?

Certainly minorities were targets of subprime lenders because they were viewed as less educated and economically disadvantaged. This is especially true of the Hispanic community where language was an additional barrier to the financial world of mortgage loans. Smooth talking bi-lingual mortgage brokers put many unsuspecting borrowers into subprime loans. With few options for acquiring a loan, minorities like Hispanics often found subprime their only option.

It's not just honest hardworking people who are victims of the subprime mess. Many innocent and ignorant homeowners have been preyed upon.

Let's examine a few scams and frauds.

Chapter 10
Frauds and Scams

"The safest way to double your money is to fold it over once and put it in your pocket."
-Kin Hubbard

A friend of mine told me a story where an investor, who was purchasing a rehab property to fix up and flip, was encouraged to falsify the mortgage application and say that the property was going to be owner occupied. The encouragement came from the mortgage broker and the real estate agent. They said things like:

- No one ever checks on it.

- You'll get a better rate that way.

- I can't get you the rate I quoted you unless it is owner occupied.

- It's all right to say it is owner occupied because everyone does it.

Apparently this isn't an isolated case. But this type of falsification is only the tip of the iceberg.

When people are in financial trouble they are vulnerable to predators and scam artists.

Here's a scam that can take several forms when a homeowner falls behind on their mortgage.

Either someone contacts the homeowner or the homeowner finds someone who helps people in 'financial trouble'. The sales pitch is that they'll help them stay in their home by buying the house and then renting it back to them with an option to buy it back. The scammers will only make that offer if there is equity in the home. The goal of this scam is to steal the equity in the home from the homeowner.

Here are three examples of different forms this scam can take.

- In the first form of this scam, the company offering the help will get the homeowner to sign over the home or sign a power of attorney. Once the scammers have that they immediately refinance the home – the scammers are hoping for as close to 100% financing as possible. After refinancing the scammers sell the home back to the homeowner and the homeowner is current on their mortgage payments. The new mortgage is usually a low introductory teaser rate so the new payment will be close to the old payment, even though the new mortgage is for much more money. Meanwhile the scammer has all the equity in the property. If the homeowner won't buy it back at the higher price the scam artist just doesn't make payments and the house goes into foreclosure. If the scammer has power of attorney, they don't have to do anything but walk away because the original owner still owns the home. Either way, the homeowner has lost all their equity.

Here are some numbers to put it in perspective. The homeowner has lived in their house for 10 years and only owes $100,000 on the mortgage and the home is worth $250,000. The homeowner has $150,000 in equity. The scam company then refinances the loan and pockets the equity. If they can get 100% financing they'll walk away with $150,000 (less refinancing fees) leaving the homeowner with a $250,000 mortgage and no equity.

- In the second form of this scam a company has an appraiser willing to falsify the appraisal. The scammer might get an appraisal for more than the home is worth, say $350,000. If so they'll try to finance it for the higher amount when they sell it back to the homeowner. If they're successful with 100% financing on the new higher appraisal they stand to take another $100,000 out of the property when selling it back to the homeowner. I know this sounds too horrible to be true, but it happens.

- The third twist on this scam is to get a third party involved who will purchase the home 'as an investment'. In reality they are doing the same thing as the scam company. Purchasing the home for the amount due on the mortgage and refinancing it. This form of the scam typically involves a mortgage broker. The broker doesn't want the home in their name because it would seem too obvious it was a scam so they get a third party to put it in their name. After the refinancing the third party either sells it back to the homeowner for the new mortgage amount or they simply don't make the payments and the house goes into foreclosure. Either way the homeowner loses the house and equity because of their ignorance.

Yes, innocent people have lost their homes due to scam artists and con men but some of the blame rests on the homeowner. A home is a huge investment. For most people it is the single largest purchase they'll ever make. The homeowner needs to have qualified, independent legal counsel review the documents before signing anything. It is the homeowner's responsibility to be certain they understand everything they are signing.

While there are legitimate companies that help people keep their home, they all make their money by taking equity out of the house. Because of the high degree of risk involved, even a legitimate company will want a huge portion of the equity to help the homeowner.

As with the second form of the previously mentioned scam, inflated appraisals have been a central part of many frauds and scams.

Suppose a homeowner wants to refinance their mortgage but doesn't have enough equity. An inflated appraisal will solve that problem.

Another example of an inflated appraisal scam involves the seller who sells for an inflated price and rebates the difference between the true market value and the inflated price to the buyer. The buyer either pockets the money and doesn't make the payments resulting in foreclosure or uses to the money to make payments while they try to sell the house. Either way, the buyer is covered because they've taken cash out of the deal up front. Worst case, they can't sell the house and when the cash they took out of the deal up-front runs out the house ends up in foreclosure. Meanwhile, they've had a place to live. This scam has been used on ordinary as well as expensive homes. If it is widespread, and the homes are sold again and again it can greatly inflate the true value of the entire neighborhood because comparable sales prices are used to determine the value of the home during the appraisal process. This made national headlines when it happened in an Atlanta suburb. Dozens of homes were sold with inflated appraisals.

Here's an example of the numbers for a $1 million home inflated to $1.5 million because of a dishonest appraisal.

- Original value of the home and the amount due on the mortgage $1 million.

- Inflated appraisal valued the home at $1.5 million.

- Refinance 90% of the value of $1.5 million means a new loan for $1.35 million with cash back of $350,000 at closing.

- A $1.35 million loan at 7% costs less than $10,000 per month.

- With $350,000 the scammers will have enough money to pay the mortgage for 35 months. That should be long enough to sell the property. If they sell in less than 35 months they keep whatever they didn't spend of the $350,000 plus they got to live in a $1 million home.

- Who knows, maybe they'll sell it for more than the $1.35 million they owe on it and they'll get to keep that profit as well.

- Maybe they don't want to spend any of that $350,000 to make mortgage payments. They just want to live in the house until they are evicted through foreclosure.

You can see why the inflated appraisal scam is so attractive and so widespread.

Because it so prevalent many financial institutions no longer allow just any appraiser on a loan, they have an approved appraiser list. That's their list of appraisers who they believe will provide a true market value appraisal.

Other financial institutions have their own in-house appraisal adjusters. They go out after an appraisal has been completed and adjust the appraisal, typically downward, to reflect the true market value of the home.

It's not just scam artists that were inflating appraisals. At the height of the subprime frenzy, financial institutions wanted the deals to go through so badly they were pressuring the appraisers to increase the value of the appraisals. Appraisers who didn't play along got blacklisted.

Now the opposite it happening, whether it is because the appraiser wants to be conservative or because they are getting pressure from the financial institution, appraisals are coming in unexpectedly low.

As of March 2008, Fannie Mae and Freddie Mac agreed to abide by the "Home Valuation Code of Conduct" that prohibits this type of appraisal activity (7).

Here's another popular scam. The scam artist finds someone with a good credit rating (good enough to get a mortgage) but not a lot of cash – we'll call this person the buyer. The scammer convinces the buyer that they will help them to buy a house with no money down. The scammer will find a house with a big difference between the asking price and the appraisal. The scammer will find a mortgage broker or lender to loan as close to 100% of the appraised price as possible. If the lender needs to see some assets in the buyer's name, the scammer will deposit money in a new bank account that the scammer and buyer setup – with restricted access so only the scammer can withdraw money – that is so the buyer can't take the scammer's money. At closing the bank funds the sale and the asking price goes to the seller and the difference between the asking price and the amount of the loan (as close to 100% of the appraised value as a financial institution is willing to loan the buyer) goes to the new bank account.

Yes it's true that the buyer gets to live in the house with no money down. However, they might not be able make the mortgage payments on a house with a mortgage higher than the asking price. The scammer doesn't care. They took the money and ran.

Here are some numbers to clarify that scam.

- The house is listed for $150,000

- The house appraised at $200,000

- The bank is willing to finance 90%, $180,000

- The scammer deposits $20,000 in the new joint account with the buyer

- The deal closes.

- The seller gets $150,000.

- $30,000 is deposited into the new bank account. ($180,000 loan less the $150,000 asking price)

- The scammer withdraws $50,000 from the bank account. That represents the $20,000 deposited to make the deal go through and the $30,000 cash out at closing.

There are many variations on this scam. For example, the buyer may be an 'investor' and be asked to put up the $20,000 and their good credit rating in exchange for a guaranteed 10% return. Little did they know that their credit rating was being used to finance the purchase of the property. Adding insult to injury, the 'investor' gets $2,000 profit and the scammer gets $28,000.

Another example of a serious problem in the mortgage process is the 'no-doc' loan. Essentially the lender says to the borrower, for a fee we'll trust whatever you tell us. It's easy to look back and say 'what were they thinking'?

Many homeowners were convinced they could afford more home than was possible and they used the no-doc loan to get the mortgage. While the interest rates were low and the housing market was appreciating rapidly this worked for many buyers.

Chapter 11
A Typical Subprime Situation

"If it isn't the sheriff, it's the finance company: I've got more attachments on me than a vacuum cleaner."
-John Barrymore

Not all subprime loans involve scams. Many hardworking people just got caught up in the idea of ever-increasing home prices and decided to get on the bandwagon.

Let's walk through an example with a fictitious couple, Joe Lack and Sue Reason. Lack and Reason are recently married, just out of college, working as schoolteachers and want to buy a home.

Lack & Reason make pretty good money; together they earn $60,000 per year. Their parents gave them $10,000 as a graduation present, which when combined with their savings will provide them with a $15,000 down payment.

They did their research and found that the rule of thumb is they shouldn't have a mortgage (principal, interest, taxes & insurance) larger than 28% of their income. At an interest rate of 6.5% they figured they could afford a $200,000 house.

The finances would look something like this:

House value: $200,000

Loan value: $185,000

Monthly Principal & Interest: $1,250

Monthly Prop Tax & Insurance: $250

Total monthly payment = $1,500

At 6.5% interest their monthly payment of $1,500 is close to the guideline of 28% of their combined total monthly income of $5,000. They thought it would be a stretch but they wanted to live in a house and start building equity. They looked at several houses in the $200,000 range and found several they liked. Granted the homes were older and needed some work, sort of fixer uppers. They weren't large; most were 2 bedrooms and one and a half baths. None of them had a garage. They were a little further out of town so they'd have a longer commute. But hey, they had to start somewhere.

Unfortunately, as recent college graduates they didn't have a high enough credit score to qualify for a prime loan through their bank. They really wanted a house instead of an apartment and they had enough money for a down payment so they decided to go to a mortgage broker to see if the broker could find them a loan.

The mortgage broker convinced Lack & Reason that they could afford a larger house by taking a subprime loan that has a low 2.5% interest rate. For the first 2 years they have 2.5% rate and then their loan adjusts to a higher rate of 8.5%. Before the higher rate takes effect they can refinance to a prime loan with a fixed or adjustable rate or another loan with an ultra low teaser rate. If they sign up for this 2.5% loan they can in fact afford a lot more home – around $300,000. The finances would look something like this:

House value: $300,000

Loan value: $285,000

Monthly Principal & Interest: $1,128

Monthly Prop Tax & Insurance: $372

Total monthly payment = $1,500

At 2.5% interest the payment is exactly the same. Wow, how great is that. The broker convinces this couple they can afford a $300,000 house.

To help convince the couple the mortgage broker tells them that not only are interest rates going down but also housing is appreciating. In two years the house will appreciate 10% per year so it will be worth $363,000. They are amazed! How does that work? The first year they get 10% appreciation so the house is worth an extra $30,000 or $330,000. The second year they earn 10% on $330,000 or $33,000. Add those together and you get $363,000. They'll earn as much by living in the house as they do by working. Isn't that amazing.

But wait, it gets better. With $63,000 of appreciation not only will they be able to refinance, but also they'll be able to get cash out. How? Well with $63,000 of appreciation and a $15,000 down payment they'll have $78,000 of equity in the house. If they pay their bills on-time for the next two years, they'll have a good credit rating and they'll qualify for a prime loan and get a great rate at 90% of the current value of the home. The current value is $363,000 and 90% of that is $326,000. Since they only owe $285,000 on the loan they could get $40,000 cash back at their refinance! Just come back in two years and the mortgage broker will put them in that loan. Can it get any better than this?

The broker told them they'd be crazy not to spend $300,000 on a house. They can't lose and after all, he's a professional. This is his business and he knows what he's talking about.

In fact, if they wanted a $400,000 house the broker said he knew a way they could afford it, at 10% appreciation that would be $84,000 in equity. This is the way people get rich. Get the biggest house you can afford on a teaser rate and refinance a couple of years down the road. So the broker explained how they could afford a $400,000 house. It works like this. The loan is called an option ARM or 'pick a payment'. Basically Lack & Reason could pay $1,500 per month for a $400,000 house and whatever they didn't pay on their loan each month would be added to the balance of what they owe on the loan. The finances would look something like this:

House value: $400,000

Loan value: $385,000

Monthly Principal & Interest: $1,521

Monthly Prop Tax & Insurance: $479

Total monthly payment due = $2,000

Total monthly payment actually paid = $1,500

Monthly amount added to loan balance = $500

Each year they'd add only $6,000 to their mortgage balance. With 10% appreciation they'd realize a net gain of $34,000 the first year. How? The $400,000 home would appreciate $40,000 the first year but they'd owe an additional $6,000 so they'd realize a net gain of $34,000 ($40,000 less $6,000) the first year and $38,000 the second year ($44,000 less $6,000 they owe for not being able to pay the extra $500 they owe each month).

Why not go for a $400,000 home?

Lack & Reason went home that night and talked it over. Wow, a $400,000 home. They could get 4 or 5 bedrooms and it would probably be new! It would have a garage, a beautiful yard, perhaps granite counters (even their parents didn't have granite counters) and be closer to work. They'd be able to save money on gasoline by not having to drive as far.

They called the broker the first thing the next morning and told him they decided to go for it with a $400,000 loan. He said he'd have the loan commitment that afternoon and they could come in and sign the papers the next day. So they showed up the next day, it was very exciting. They had to sign a bunch of papers, so many papers that they didn't really read them all because it would've taken a week to read everything. The broker just told them where to sign. They were so excited.

Lack & Reason spent every spare minute looking at houses. Within a week they found a new house and set a closing date.

When they got to the closing there were a couple of surprises.

First was a pre-payment penalty. If they refinance within the first 5 years they'll be subject to a 10% pre-payment penalty. Granted the pre-payment penalty declines from 10% to 0% at the rate of 2% per year but sill it wasn't what they were expecting. If they refinance within the 1st year it is 10% and within the 2nd year they'll be subject to an 8% pre-payment penalty or approximately $32,000. They need to refinance before the end of the 2nd year or they'll have an 8.5% interest rate payment and they really couldn't afford that.

Wow! That kind of ruined their plan for getting cash back. They got their mortgage broker on the phone and he said it was the best he could do given their credit rating. Oh well, they really wanted the house. They've come all this way; it would really be disappointing to walk away now. Hey, they can always refinance later on. Let's go for it.

Second was something called a '<u>yield spread premium</u>' of 2%. It looked like an $8,000 charge that Lack & Reason were going to have to pay to the bank or mortgage broker at closing. Granted they wouldn't have to write a check for it but it would be added to their mortgage balance. Instead of having a mortgage balance of $385,000 it looked like it was going to be closer to $400,000 by the time the yield spread premium and the closing costs were added to the mortgage balance. All of their $15,000 in down payment would be eaten up in fees! They called mortgage broker and he said it was the best he could do given their credit rating.

Since they didn't get a satisfactory answer from the mortgage broker about what the yield spread premium was they asked the closing attorney. The attorney said that generally the yield spread premium is a payment to the mortgage broker from the financial institution for directing the customer to them. Essentially it is a commission payment.

What? That's right, it seems the mortgage broker steered Lack & Reason to a loan with a pre-payment penalty so that he could get a bigger yield spread premium.

The financial institution is confident they'll make back the money they paid in commission because of the pre-payment penalty.

The mortgage broker is already getting a 1% commission or $4,000. He was able to arrange the loan that same day and Lack & Reason signed the loan commitment papers the next day. The mortgage broker had a bunch of people in his office the same day Lack & Reason were there so you know he was able to process more than one loan per day. Seems like $4,000 was a lot to pay for a few hours work, but $12,000 is outrageous.

Let's review the new picture of the finances. Rather than refinance $385,000, Lack & Reason will need to refinance $444,000. What!? How did it get to be $444,000?

- $400,000 loan value

- Plus $32,000 pre-payment penalty

- Plus $12,000 for the $500 that was added to the mortgage balance each month because their payment didn't cover the cost of the loan).

This deal is not exactly what the mortgage broker promised. Lack & Reason really didn't want to sign the papers. They really didn't want to give the mortgage broker $12,000. They really didn't want a $444,000 financial obligation. But they'd already paid their $300 mortgage application fee and they didn't want to lose that. They really liked the house and didn't want to lose that. They'd already told their friends about their new house. So, they signed.

Does this sound familiar? Unfortunately it is for far too many people. They were lead to believe one thing by their mortgage broker only to get to closing and find something else.

So what will happen to Lack & Reason at the end of their two-year teaser rate?

If they have 10% appreciation, what will their payment look like if they simply refinance their $444,000 obligation into a prime loan at 6.5%? We'll use a $444,000 number to be conservative, even though with closing costs it will probably be more like $450,000.

House value: $463,000

Loan value: $444,000

Monthly Principal & Interest: $2,730

Monthly Prop Tax & Insurance: $479

Total monthly payment = $3,209

Unfortunately the $3,209 payment exceeds the 28% guideline by far too much for them to be able to get this type of loan. In fact, $3,209 is almost their entire take home pay! At the end of the two year 'teaser' rate they'll need to sign up for another subprime loan and incur another set of closing costs and possibly incur another pre-payment penalty. They may not even be able to get another loan because after the financial institution adds in another set of closing costs Lack & Reason may not have any equity left in the home.

Can it really cost that much to refinance? Take a look on the Internet for refinancing and read the fine print. You'll see many offers that have costs around 5% of the value of the loan. Probably the most familiar and the biggest fee on a mortgage loan are the 'points'. The less credit worthy the buyer, the higher the points they'll pay.

Here's a list of some of the fees you'll see on a mortgage closing statement:

- Real Estate Commission
- Mortgage Broker Commission
- Transfer Fees
- Loan Origination Fee
- Loan Discount Fee
- Document Preparation Fee
- Appraisal Fee
- Credit Report Fee
- Lender's Inspection Fee

- Mortgage Insurance Application Fee
- Mortgage Insurance Premium
- Hazard Insurance Premium
- Assumption Fee
- Flood Certification Fee
- Closing Fee
- Settlement Fee
- Abstract Fee
- Title Search Fee
- Title Examination Fee
- Title Insurance Binder Fee
- Title Insurance
- Notary Fee
- Attorney's Fees
- Courier Fee
- Post Closing / Handling Fee
- Release Fee
- Recording Fee

- City/County/Stamps
- State Tax/Stamps
- Survey Fee
- Pest Inspection Fee

If you've signed a mortgage contract take a moment to dig it up and look for yourself. It isn't uncommon to pay 1% in fees plus whatever the mortgage broker gets (say 3%) plus whatever the real estate broker gets (say 6%) plus whatever the financial institution gets (points – say 2%). If you live where they have a transfer tax you'll also have several thousand in fees there (say 2%). Add them all up and you get 14%. Now that is a lot of fees!

Not all of these fees are going to be on every closing statement. Also, the buyer does not pay all the fees; the seller pays some, but they are paid.

Even if this loan didn't have a pre-payment penalty, there is no way this couple could afford this house with a prime rate loan. At this rate they'll go from subprime loan to subprime loan and never get out from under this burden unless they sell the house.

Now what happens if they don't see 10% per year appreciation? Suppose they don't have any appreciation at all! Let's see what the financial picture looks like.

House value: $400,000

Loan value: $444,000

Oh no! Lack & Reason owe more than the house is worth! How did this happen. It sounded so good when the mortgage broker was talking about the financial numbers. No wonder he's not returning their calls. In order to refinance Lack & Reason will need to come up with money for a down payment and money for closing costs because those can no longer be added to the mortgage balance. They don't have any savings because they used it to buy the house! There isn't a bank out there that will loan them money on home in which they don't have any equity. What are they going to do? They can't borrow from their parents; they are living on social security and gave them most of their savings as a graduation gift for a down payment.

Ok, so they still own the home. Maybe they can somehow afford to live in it without refinancing.

Let's see what their payment will looks like when it adjusts to 8.5%. Good news, they won't have a pre-payment penalty to refinance but they'll still have the $12,000 added to the mortgage balance for the $500 per month they couldn't afford to pay at the beginning of the loan.

House value: $400,000

Loan value: $412,000

Monthly Principal & Interest: $3,218

Monthly Prop Tax & Insurance: $479

Total monthly payment = $3,697

Let's examine this as a percentage increase to get a better feel for what's really happening. A 6% increase in the interest rate, plus changing from the $1,500 payment to what they'll actually owe on the loan - $3,697 - means a

146% increase in their payment. Could you afford a 146% increase in your mortgage? Even if we examine it from what was actually owed each month - $2,000 – it still represents an 85% increase in their mortgage payment.

Why didn't the financial professionals involved with this transaction make Lack & Reason aware of this possibility? The simple answer is greed. Of course interest rates could have fallen and for many years they did. Of course home prices could have continued to climb and for many years they did. But, how many subprime borrowers were counseled about what would happen if interest rates rose and/or home prices didn't appreciate?

Unfortunately there is no way they can pay $3,697 per month because that is more than they take home in their paychecks – let alone their car payments, electricity, gas, cable, Internet, food, insurance, water, phone, etc. etc. etc.

Lack & Reason are depressed. Their dreams are crushed. They are financially ruined. They'll lose the house. They'll lose their down payment and equity. They'll lose their good credit rating. It will be a long time before they'll be able to afford another house. First they'll have to save at least $15,000. If they can save $500 a month it will take them two and half years to save $15,000. They'll need at least that long to repair their credit rating after losing the house. Lack & Reason will want to save more than $15,000 so that they move into the house with some savings just in case.

Looking back they wonder what would've happened if they had decided to go for the $300,000 house instead. The loan value would've been $300,000 because the mortgage broker commission and closing costs ate up all of their $15,000 down payment. Can they afford a $300,000 house after two years when their rate adjusts? Here's what it looks like at 8.5%

House value: $300,000

Loan value: $300,000

Monthly Principal & Interest: $2,343

Monthly Prop Tax & Insurance: $372

Total monthly payment = $2,715

Unfortunately, this monthly payment is over 50% of their monthly income and they won't be able to find a financial institution to give them a loan for that large a payment.

OK, what about refinancing to a prime loan at 6.5%? They'll still have the pre-payment penalty as well as the mortgage broker commission and closing costs that ate up their down payment so they'll need to refinance $324,000 plus estimated closing costs of $6,000 or $330,000 without appreciation.

House value: $300,000

Loan value: $330,000

Again, there isn't a financial institution out there that will refinance a home with a loan for more than it is worth. The only option is to be stuck with a payment of $2,715 per month. That is almost their entire take home pay.

Maybe they can make it if they live off their credit cards, stop contributing to their retirement funds, borrow

Page 88   Subprime

money from their life insurance and save every penny. Unfortunately, even that won't be enough.

They couldn't even afford the $300,000 house. What were they thinking buying a $400,000 house?

OK, what would've happened if they had bought that $200,000 home at the 2.5% teaser rate?

First, let's see what the finances would look like by refinancing at 6.5%.

After the two-year period they'll need to pay the prepayment penalty of 8% or $16,000 plus estimated closing costs of $5,000 for a total of $21,000. If they have 10% appreciation they're in good shape.

House value: $242,000

Loan value: $221,000

Monthly Principal & Interest: $1,396

Monthly Prop Tax & Insurance: $250

Total monthly payment = $1,646

While the payment has gone up by about 10% their incomes will have hopefully gone up by 5% per year so they're in pretty good shape. They've got a 30-year loan at a fixed rate that is reasonably affordable. Hopefully they won't have a layoff, illness or other catastrophe that jeopardizes their income.

What would happen if there weren't 10% appreciation? Here's what those numbers look like.

House value: $200,000

Loan value: $221,000

No financial institution is going to loan them money on a property with negative equity.

So what do we learn from this. Lack & Reason couldn't even afford to refinance the $200,000 home without 10% per year appreciation and even that would be a stretch. For them to receive guidance from a mortgage broker that they could afford more home was wrong. He should have known they couldn't afford a $400,000 home.

Why would the mortgage broker do this? The simple answer is money. The mortgage broker has no financial exposure. He doesn't care whether Lack & Reason kept the house or not. He made his money and was paid at closing. The commission and yield-spread premium took care of him and he was on to his next deal.

Why would the financial institution make this loan? The answer isn't quite as simple as the motivation for the mortgage broker. The financial institution is interested in making money but also, thanks to our Congress, they have a legal obligation to make loans to less creditworthy people. After the closing, the financial institution will bundle the loan with other loans and sell it on the open market through securitization. Once they've sold the loan they have no financial exposure.

Three questions come to mind.

1. How did we get to this point in America?

2. How did the great American dream of home ownership bring so many people to financial ruin?

3. What can we do to make certain this doesn't happen again?

    I'll try to answer those questions for you, but first, let's look at the role of credit rating agencies.

Chapter 12
Credit Rating Agencies

"He that is of the opinion money will do everything may well be suspected of doing everything for money."
-Benjamin Franklin

The role of credit rating agencies in the subprime market is interesting. There can be no question that some of the burden of blame for the current crisis rests with the credit rating agencies.

I'm not suggesting this crisis is entirely their fault. But they were handing out triple A rating for subprime bonds like candy. They seriously underestimated the risk involved with these loans and securities.

In their defense, when the Mortgage Backed Securities were carved up and the worst performing loans placed in the Special Purpose Vehicles it became nearly impossible to accurately predict the overall performance of the loan portfolio.

In August 2007 as the credit problems came to a head, many investors saw the rating on their investments go from the very best credit rating to default in a day or two.

Investments that were sold as low risk went into default without warning. There are many money managers who purchased these investments because they carried an excellent rating and appeared to be low risk.

Many investors are asking how their investments could go from excellent to default in such a short period of time. They are also asking how insured bonds become worthless.

The answer goes back to the complexity of the investment. Because of the separation between the asset and the mortgage-backed securities, it is possible for the bonds to become worthless even as the underlying asset maintained most of its value.

We also had bonds downgraded which results in immediate devaluation. The losses for downgraded bonds are also enormous.

What will change at credit rating agencies as a result of the subprime fiasco? I anticipate there will be:

- Lawsuits about these issues for years to come.

- Changes in the Bond & Credit rating business as a result of the subprime meltdown. Perhaps they will take the initiative and make the changes themselves or perhaps congress or another governmental agency will mandate the changes.

- There will be management changes at the credit rating agencies. Heads will roll as a result of the misinterpretation of the risks involved.

One thing is for certain. The credit rating business will never be the same again.

Chapter 13
The Forecast

"Economists report that a college education adds many thousands of dollars to a man's lifetime income - which he then spends sending his son to college."
-Bill Vaughn

Before it's over, I believe the subprime losses will total many trillions of dollars and result in a 25% to 30% decline in the value of the American housing market.

Let's examine the numbers behind those forecasts. I've heard a variety numbers for the quantity of mortgages that are in foreclosure, but let's say 2 million households are in foreclosure and 5 million are delinquent.

In addition to the people who have been foreclosed or are delinquent, there are repercussions in other areas of the economy. There will be many industries that are negatively impacted by a downturn in the housing market. For example:

- People in the mortgage closing business (mortgage brokers, processors, appraisers, title search & insurance, lawyers etc.)

- People in the financial services sector (50,000 layoffs as of May 2008)

- People involved in the construction business. By the time you include all the subcontractors it takes well over 100 people to build a house and if you are in a hurry and have the money the number of people goes up dramatically.

- People who provide products to the home building business (concrete, lumber, drywall, electrical fixtures, plumbing, HVAC, roofing, insulation, siding, windows, doors, flooring, granite, appliances, home furnishings, etc.)

- These are just a few examples; the impact is far and wide.

How does all of that translate into dollars and cents?

Our Gross Domestic Product – everything we sell – is around $14 trillion. I've heard that the housing market is responsible for about 5% of that. If we add all of the other people listed above I think we could reasonably double that number to 10% of our GDP or $1.4 trillion represents the value of people associated with the home building business. I've read recently that housing starts are down by 25%. If this $1.4 trillion industry experiences a 25% decline that is a $350 billion impact. That's $350 billion in paychecks and profits that will disappear. Those people won't be able to buy things (cars, TVs, computers and maybe not even food) that contribute to our overall GDP and employ others. The impact goes many levels deep, not just the housing sector so I believe $350 billion is actually a fairly conservative estimate.

<u>The first tally of the negative impact on our economy is $350 billion.</u>

What about all the write-downs in the existing mortgages? Just reading the news over the last couple of months I've seen all the big banks and finance companies announce huge write-downs and write-offs and then come back and announce yet more write-offs and write-downs. I'm guessing about 100 subprime lenders have gone out of business and the industry has already taken about $350 billion in write-offs and it could go anywhere from $500 billion to over $1 trillion. When you consider the mortgage backed security market is over $7 trillion, a $500 billion to $1 trillion write-off represents between 7% and 14% of the market. That could turn out to be fairly conservative.

<u>The second tally of the impact is between $500 billion and $1 trillion in write-offs by financial institutions.</u>

Probably the biggest impact is that millions of homes lose value. The value will simply disappear. Of course the foreclosed homes will lose value, but so will all other homes. If there's a foreclosed home on your block it will bring your property values down as well. If you are trying to sell your house and you are competing with foreclosed homes in your area you'll get less money for your house. Banks aren't in the real estate business; they're in the money business. They don't have the staff or the inclination to manage real estate properties so they unload them as quickly as they can even if they have to take a loss.

When millions of homes are foreclosed across the country it has a devastating effect on property values.

According to the U.S. Census Bureau the value of all U.S. housing in 2006 was slightly more than $20 trillion. We have mortgages of around $14 trillion – same as the GDP. The experts tell us our problems in the subprime market and the impact on the housing market won't be fully known for another two years. In the last two years the value of all U.S. housing is down 16%, and most of that decline has happened in the last 12 months. If the value of all U.S. housing were to decline 25% it would wipe out virtually all the equity people hold in their homes. Along with lost equity the homeowners have also lost access to additional credit through home equity loans.

Given the rapid decline in housing prices in recent months a 25% decline over the next couple of years isn't hard to fathom.

If the economy goes into recession 25% could be fairly conservative. So, if our housing values decline by 25%, it means a loss of $5 trillion in the value of our homes. With a loss of equity in our homes also comes a loss of access to credit, primarily through home equity loans.

<u>The third tally of the impact is $5 trillion in lost housing value.</u>

The final impact is on people's attitude toward spending. The economists measure this via the Consumer Confidence Index. The index measures people's attitude toward their future employment and income prospects. In 2008 consumer confidence is at a 28 year low.

What this means for the economy is:

- People might not take that vacation
- They might not buy that new car
- They might not buy that new big screen TV
- The list goes on and on.

The result for just those examples above is a long list of people who are negatively impacted by the <u>expectation</u> of not having as much future income.

For example, if just one person cancels their vacation plans here's a list of people and companies that might make less income.

- Vacation rental company
- The vacation rental staff
- The vacation destination restaurants
- The resort rental companies
- The airlines
- The rental car companies
- The department stores that sell vacation clothing
- The vacation golf course
- The vacation entertainment companies
- The vacation insurance company
- The list goes on and on....

You get the idea. Negative consumer confidence means we spend less and the reach is far and wide.

The impact of negative consumer confidence could easily exceed $1 trillion.

Let's add up all the lost income, revenue and value:

Home building & related industries	$0.35 trillion
Financial institutions (average)	$0.75 trillion
Value of U.S. homes	$5.00 trillion
Consumer Confidence	$1.00 trillion
Total	$7.10 trillion

$7.1 trillion total equals approximately 50% of the U.S. GDP.

I think this puts the economists' concerns in perspective. However, this number is so large I can't wrap my mind around it $7,100,000,000,000. I need to understand it by comparing to something.

To put it in perspective let's say we invested that $7.1 trillion in the stock market. The average annual return in the stock market has been around 10%. Our $7.1 trillion investment in the stock market would return $710 billion annually. The Federal Government collected $1,100 billion in individual income taxes in 2007. We would *earn* almost as much as the Federal Government.

That number is still too large for me to get a handle on it. Let's say you have a regular 40-hour per week job. Just the interest you earn in your investment, $710 billion annually would be equal to:

- $591 million per month
- $136 million per week
- $27 million per day
- $3.4 million per hour

$3.4 million per hour is the equivalent of one hundred $34,000 cars – every hour. I think that puts it in perspective. And that is just the gain from the stock market – we're not talking about the principal.

Think about what you could do with $3.4 million per hour. How many homeless people could be housed and fed? Answer, all of them! How many jobs could be created? How many bridges built? How many worthwhile causes could be supported? You'd have over $27 million each and every workday just on the gains that $7.1 trillion earns in the stock market.

So what's the bottom line? This is a great deal of value to remove from our economic system.

Are my estimates too high? Even if I'm 50% too high, it still represents an enormous blow to the U.S. economy.

But what if I'm 50% too low? These are fairly conservative estimates. These estimates only include the subprime market. What happens if it spreads to the Alt-A market, the group just above subprime? That could mean 5 million foreclosures. 5 million foreclosures would mean a loss in value equal to one year of the U.S. GDP - $14 trillion.

I've heard people say there is no way we could have 5 million foreclosures. I disagree. We have a 16% decline in the value of homes across the U.S. Everyone who purchased a home last year and put down 15% or less (the average down payment is probably less than 10%) is living in a home that is worth less than the mortgage– also known as 'negative equity'. This means that more than 5 million homes have negative equity. Perhaps that explains why 5 million homeowners are delinquent on their mortgages. This is a recipe for disaster because the incentive is for those people to default on their mortgage, abandon the property and start over. It is already happening in markets that have had steep declines in the value of homes.

In addition to the buyers in the last 12 months who have had their equity erased we could add everyone who put 10% or less down during the past 24-36 months. Now we're talking about more than 10 million homeowners with 'negative equity' - again owing more than their home is worth.

If the average value of the U.S. home declines 30% we'll have more than 20 million homeowners with negative equity. In the event we have 20 million homeowners with negative equity we face a grave situation. Remember there are 80 million homeowners in the U.S. so 20 million with negative equity would represent 25% of all homeowners.

Many of those homeowners will choose to exit their financial bind through a short sale or default and abandon the property. In a short sale the homeowner will sell the property for whatever they can, which will be much less than what is owed on the property. The financial institution agrees in advance to forgive the rest to avoid foreclosure. In the event this does happen it will put downward pressure on home prices pushing more homeowners into a negative equity situation. This is a viscous cycle that could spiral to

30 million, 40 million even 50 million homeowners with a 30%, 40% even 50% decline in value of the average U.S. home.

Hopefully we've already seen the bottom, the worst is over and we are on our way to recovery and prosperity.

I believe the American economy is one of the strongest in the world. I believe in the free-market system. I believe we will recover from this financial crisis, and yes it is a crisis. I still believe the best way for the average American to accumulate wealth is through home ownership.

Nevertheless, this is an incredibly serious problem for our economy.

Chapter 14
Where Do We Go From Here?

"If you owe the bank $100 that's your problem. If you owe the bank $100 million, that's the bank's problem."

-JP Getty

We need to address three issues.

- First we need to address the issue of foreclosures.

- Second we need to address the underlying financial issues surrounding the liquidity and credit crisis so this doesn't happen again.

- Third we need to make loans more transparent so that people can understand the extent of the financial obligation they are agreeing to by signing their mortgage documents. This will probably only happen through legislation.

Let's look at the foreclosure issue.

Some people have suggested that Fannie Mae and Freddie Mac should rescue subprime borrowers. There have been a number of proposals including:

- Raising the loan limits

- Doing away with the 20% downpayment requirement

- Increasing the dollar limit on their loan portfolios

- Underwriting or assuming existing subprime mortgages

I believe using Fannie Mae and/or Freddie Mac to address this crisis is the wrong approach. First these are government sponsored companies but still privately owned shareholder companies. As taxpayers we already contribute $10 billion to these companies. Our government shouldn't be responsible for bailing out the entire private sector mortgage problem. These companies have their own problems. Fannie Mae reported a $1.4 billion loss for Q3 2007 and it has $75 billion in loans that are rated below prime. Both Fannie & Freddie are being investigated by the New York Attorney General.

Some people have suggested a federal bailout of failed mortgages. In 2007 the U.S. Treasury took in $1.8 trillion in total tax receipts (personal income taxes, business taxes, social security taxes, etc) and the federal government spent $2.8 trillion. We are already spending $1 trillion more than we take in. Can we really afford to bail out 2 million foreclosed homes?

Another suggestion to keep our economy from spiraling downward out of control has been to put an immediate freeze on foreclosures. However, I believe all that does is delay the day of reckoning and market correction.

One option I do support would be to change the terms of all ARMs that are about to adjust. This is a slippery slope but one that hopefully we can navigate. When the teaser rate expires, rather than adjust to the typical rate of prime or LIBOR plus 5% we could adjust it to the prime rate or prime plus 1%. There are several problems with this approach but it has the potential to help us avoid a meltdown in the housing and financial markets.

What are the problems with this approach?

- The first problem is having the government modify private sector contracts. That doesn't sit well with me and I'm sure it doesn't sit well with our financial institutions. If the government can modify mortgage contracts why not let them modify any contract.

- The second problem is the negative impact on our financial institutions, they'll have to forego the higher interest rates. One could argue that they'll come out ahead in the end because they won't have to foreclose on as many homes.

- Another problem is the moral hazard. For future decisions it encourages additional risk taking because the government bailed out the borrower this time so they'll do it in the future. Not a good precedent to set.

- Holding the increase of the adjustable rate mortgages to prime or prime plus 1% is unfair to those borrowers who had ARM's and refinanced those loans. Those who refinanced had to pay additional costs that borrowers under this proposal won't have to pay. If they had known their rate was going to be adjusted to prime they probably wouldn't have refinanced. How are we going to balance the financial impact between these two groups?

- What about all those people who have already lost their home to foreclosure?

- It only delays the day reckoning for all those who purchased more house than they could afford.

Is this the only approach? Certainly not. Is this the best approach? Probably not. I'm sure there are other approaches that would work just as well if not better. However, subprime borrowers are probably the least able to afford the prime + 5%. By adjusting their rate to prime plus 1% it gives subprime borrowers the best chance of keeping their homes.

This approach also avoids a federal 'bailout' like the Savings and Loan fiasco – which cost taxpayers $250 billion. You'll recall that disaster was allowed to mushroom out of control because our Congress decided it would be in the best interest of the public to allow savings and loans to invest in a wide variety of investments for which they had no experience – derivatives etc. The congressional approval rating is at an all-time low of around 18% for a reason. Do you really trust Congress to spend your money wisely?

There are other steps the need to be taken to contain this problem but this is a good start.

So what can we do to fix the underlying problems.

The first thing that needs to be done is to stop allowing the use of Special Purpose Vehicles to remove the risk from the accounting records of our financial institutions that are creating the CDO's.

Congress is proposing a law (several laws actually regarding the subprime meltdown), The Mortgage Reform and Anti-Predatory Lending Act, that will hold lenders liable for loaning money to people that can't repay it. This Act will hold the lenders liable after they sell the mortgage. This is a lawyers dream. They'll have a field day suing every financial institution in America. Anyone that isn't able to make their mortgage payment will be able to sue saying they were sold an unffordable mortage.

We need antipredatory lending laws, but holding lenders liable for loaning money to people that can't repay it isn't the answer. The first step in solving this problem is to remove the availability of easy money for subprime borrowers from the system. That's what Georgia did with the Fair Lending Act and the federal government over-ruled them.

- In 2002 Georgia passed the Fair Lending Act. Basically the law said that any company that purchased loans that were deemed to be predatory could be held liable.

- It was virtually impossible to tell which subprime loans were predatory so the secondary market stopped purchasing subprime loans. When the sources of funds disappeared, financial institutions stopped making subprime loans in Georgia.

- This was Georgia's way of protecting subprime borrowers and New York, New Jersey and New Mexico were in the process of passing the same type of law when the federal government intervened.

- At the request of the banking industry the Office of the Comptroller of the Currency, a Federal Institution, ruled that the Georgia law was in conflict with Federal Law and could not be applied to National Banks. Because that would give National Banks an unfair advantage over local banks, the legistlation was killed.

- The Office of the Comptroller of the Currency issued a statement to the effect of 'we know how to deal with predatory lending'. In retrospect they were obviously wrong.

The second thing we need to do to solve the underlying problem is to stop requiring our financial institutions to loan money to uncreditworthy borrowers.

The Treasury has worked with our largest institutional investors to create a superfund to purchase CDO's. To me this looks like throwing good money after bad. We don't know the value of those CDO's. We need to let the market settle down and have all the facts come out before we start a rescue plan. A rescue will just encourage this type of behavior in the future.

Congress is currently proposing legislation that would allow banks to dump several hundred billion dollars worth of bad loans on the FHA. The overall cost of the proposed legislation is over $300 billion. The only thing it will accomplish it to bail out the most irresponsible among us – both banks and borrowers – and saddle the average American with the bill via higher taxes.

Finally, we need to make the true cost of a mortgage more transparent. Here are some of the ways we could do that.

1. We should clearly enumerate the broker's commission and make it illegal for financial institutions to pay a broker any money beyond what the consumer has agreed to as commission in advance (i.e. eliminate the yield spread premium-YSP). There is more than enough profit in these loans to pay commissions to the brokers. We don't' need to pay brokers double commissions. Besides the YSP presents a conflict of interest for the broker – do they want to do what is best for the customer or do they want to make a bigger commissions. Guess which way many chose to close.

2. We should require all financial institutions to verify income. No more no-doc loans.

3. We should make it illegal to charge borrowers excessive points & fees. Any loan that has fees exceeding 5% of the value of the loan is outrageous and should be illegal. There is more than enough money to be made in the lending business. Financial institutions don't need to gouge borrowers with excessive fees.

4. We should eliminate all pre-payment penalties. The primary reason for a pre-payment penalty (other than gouging consumers for additional profit on an already highly profitable transaction) is to insure the

bank will recover the commission paid to the mortgage broker via the yield spread premium. There are more than enough fees on a mortgage without adding the pain of the pre-payment penalty when it comes time to refinance or sell. If we did away with the yield spread premium, financial institutions wouldn't need prepayment penalties to recapture pre-paid commissions.

5. We should limit the number of unnecessary items that can be added to a closing statement. Some brokers sell unnecessary home warranties and other products to unsuspecting borrowers. Sometimes these figures are all lumped together under closing costs so that the buyer has a hard time seeing exactly what they're getting. If they want to purchase these types of products after closing they are free to do so. My guess is that once the light of truth shines on many of these products few if any customers will opt to purchase them.

6. We should better educate borrowers. I've heard that some brokers will encourage borrowers to refinance a loan in order to lower the interest rate on their mortgage by as little as ¼% point, just so the broker can make additional money in fees. That's outrageous!

Chapter 15
What Conclusions Can Be Drawn?

"The hardest thing in the world to understand is income tax."
-Albert Einstein

Booms and busts are part of the business cycle. Be prepared.

In real estate this means putting 20% down in cash so that you don't end up owing more than the house is worth. If the house was a fair deal when you bought it then in the long run it will be a good investment even if it declines in value in the short term.

Don't panic. Real estate values in the long run are always appreciating. There is only so much land and the population continues to grow.

Right now is a good time to buy real estate if you don't have to sell real estate to do it.

If you have real estate, and you can wait to sell, you should wait. The market will recover.

An excellent way to provide for emergency cash is to have a home equity line of credit. Get it at closing or shortly thereafter so that if the market value of your home declines you'll still have access to your line of credit. It is important that you exercise discipline and not use the line of credit unless it is an emergency, like a job loss.

Don't overload yourself with debt. Don't overextend yourself financially by assuming that times will always be good or that you'll somehow get by just because you always have until now.

- Live within your means.

- Don't buy too much house.

- Don't borrow money to invest, earn it first.

Some people have suggested this is a tipping point for housing. By that they mean that the entire industry and perhaps our economy will collapse under the weight of the subprime mess and the contraction of available credit. I disagree. The U.S. Household net worth is about $60 trillion. Even if the subprime fiasco hit $10 billion in losses that would only be about 15% of our net worth.

Don't use a mortgage broker unless you've exhausted all other options. I'll admit it, I have an ax to grind with mortgage brokers. The first time I used one was for my 4th real estate transaction. I was working in a sales organization at the time and traveling frequently. For the real estate transaction I was using a 1031 Like Kind Exchange (Starker). In that transaction you only have so many days to identify the property and close in order to be able to roll over the gains into the new property tax free. Because of my travel schedule, I decided to use a mortgage broker. I asked him to make sure of the two things:

1. I didn't want a pre-payment penalty on the loan.

2. I didn't want to see a yield spread premium, I agreed to an up front fixed fee. I didn't want to pay commission twice.

When I got to the closing surprise, surprise – there was a pre-payment penalty on the loan. I was stuck. I had to close or I'd lose my tax free exchange. In the end it only cost me a couple of bucks because my holding period was many years. Nevertheless, I got burned by the mortgage broker and of course never did business with him again. I also made sure to tell everyone I knew that they should steer clear of that company because they'll rip you off.

How does the saying go? Fool me once shame on you, fool me twice shame on me.

So about 15 years later I had an investment property in one city and I lived in a different city. I had a partner on the investment property and we needed to refinance our loan. My partner said he had a great broker (my blood pressure begins to rise) who can get us a great deal on a loan. I say I don't want to work with a broker but my partner assures me this is a great guy, a straight shooter. I said I wanted to talk with him to make sure of two things:

1. I didn't want a pre-payment penalty on the loan.

2. I didn't want to see a yield spread premium, I would agree to an up front fixed fee. I didn't want to pay commission twice.

When I talked with the broker he assured me we wouldn't have a pre-payment penalty and we wouldn't have a yield spread premium.

You guessed it. When I got to the closing there was a pre-payment penalty and a yield spread premium. I had to close. My loan we due and I needed to refinance. The yield spread premium was large enough to provide the mortgage broker with a new car. Ugh.

So where do we go from here? Is it bad? Yes. Will it get worse before it gets better? Maybe.

In the long term, the capitalist society has been the most productive of all forms of social systems. It has produced the highest standards of living and provided the most benefits to mankind.

Some people will argue that the capitalism is flawed. They argue that the market economy gets it wrong. I believe they are wrong. Wealth is power. Capitalism creates wealth so that anyone can become powerful. Capitalism provides balance and equity among trading partners. Capitalism provides rewards for the fruits of education and labor. Capitalism provides truth and conquers tyranny. Capitalism is destined to free all of mankind.

God bless America and our capitalist society. May we thrive forever.

Bibliography

(1) Home Mortgage Disclosure Act (HMDA) 1975
<http://www.ffiec.gov/hmda/>

(2) Community Reinvestment Act (CRA) 1977
<http://www.ffiec.gov/cra/history.htm>

(3) Depository Institutions Deregulatory and Monetary Control Act (DIDMCA) 1980
<http://www.fdic.gov/regulations/laws/rules/5500-700.html>

(4) Alternative Mortgage Transaction Parity Act (AMTPA) 1982
<http://www.commerce.senate.gov/public/_files/KeestTestimony.pdf>

(5) The Federal Reserve Board, Open Market Operations 1990-2008
<http://www.federalreserve.gov/fomc/fundsrate.htm>

(6) Construction & Housing: Homeownership and Housing Costs 2008
<http://www.census.gov/compendia/statab/cats/construction_housing/homeownership_and_housing_costs.html>

(7) Office of Federal Housing Enterprise Oversight March 3, 2008
<http://www.ofheo.gov/newsroom.aspx?ID=417&q1=0&q2=0>

- The U.S. Department of Treasury
  http://www.ustreas.gov

- The U.S. Department of Housing and Urban Development http://www.huduser.org
    a. Office of Policy Development and Research

- The Bureau of Economic Development
  http://www.bea.gov/

- The Federal Reserve http://www.federalreserve.gov
    a. http://www.federalreserve.gov/boarddocs/speeches/2003/20030304/default.htm
    b. http://www.federalreserve.gov/newsevents/speech/2004speech.htm
    c. http://www.federalreserve.gov/BOARDDOCS/TESTIMONY/2005/200506092/default.htm

- The U.S. Government Printing Office
  http://www.access.gpo.gov
    a. www.access.gpo.gov/congress/senate/pdf/108hrg/86497.pdf

- The New York Federal Reserve
  http://www.newyorkfed.org

- Federal Financial Institutions Examination Council
  http://www.ffiec.gov

- The U.S. Census Bureau http://www.census.gov

- The Federal Deposit Insurance Corporation
  http://www.FDIC.gov

- The U.S. Deparment of Commerce
  http://www.commerce.gov

Made in the USA
Coppell, TX
01 December 2020